THE QUARREL WITHIN

"We make out of the quarrel with others rhetoric;
but out of the quarrel with
ourselves, poetry."

William Butler Yeats

KENNIKAT PRESS

NATIONAL UNIVERSITY PUBLICATIONS

SERIES ON LITERARY CRITICISM

General Editor
EUGENE GOODHEART
Professor of Literature, Massachusetts Institute of Technology

Lawrence W. Hyman

The Quarrel Within
Art and Morality in Milton's Poetry

National University Publications
KENNIKAT PRESS
Port Washington, N. Y. / London / 1972

Library of Congress Catalog Card. No: 76-189559
ISBN: 0-8046-9018-9

Manufactured in the United States of America

Published by
Kennikat Press, Inc.
Port Washington, N.Y./London

185747

Contents

Preface

THAT THE ARTISTIC significance of Milton's poetry is quite separate from the validity of Milton's religious beliefs is a fact that has long been recognized by ordinary readers as well as by critics of Milton. It is, in fact, almost a commonplace of literary criticism to assert that we do not have to agree with Milton's doctrines in order to appreciate his poetry. But it is, or at least it should be, equally obvious that the moral doctrines of the poetry cannot be ignored. For to ignore the content of the poetry would be to trivialize the poetic experience. Just as we cannot reduce the poetry to its doctrinal content, or to its *morality,* so we cannot reduce great poetry to its *form.* To separate the form from the content of a work would be another way of saying that the work in question is not a poem at all, or at least that we no longer read it as a significant literary work.

There are, of course, many ways of resolving this problem of taking the poetry seriously without swallowing Milton's doctrine. What I propose to do here is to emphasize the difference between the doctrines that went into the poems and the moral significance that comes out of the poems. The imaginative experience of the poem is indeed permeated by a morality, but it is not a morality bound up with any set of doctrines. Something happens to the beliefs and to the feelings of Milton once these beliefs and feelings become part of the poem; and my interest will be directed to what happens in the poem, to the imaginative experience rather than to the raw doctrine.

A number of critics and readers have pointed out this disparity between what, it is alleged, Milton wanted us to feel and what in fact most readers actually feel while reading the major poems. But the disparity is generally thought of as a weakness, as a sign of Milton's failure to carry out his intention, or as a failure on the part of the reader to realize the intention. I believe, however, that far from being a weakness this disparity between the formal doctrine and reader's feelings is the source of the tension that gives the poem its distinctive power. As Yeats reminded us many years ago, it is only rhetoric that is created out of the quarrel with others; out of the quarrel with ourselves we make poetry.

To appreciate Milton's major poems, therefore, it is not necessary to divorce the art from the morality, to take the poetry and let the religion go, as many readers believe. Instead, we should see the moral philosophy in the poems no longer as dogma with which we must agree or disagree, but as an integral part of the imaginative experience. As such, Milton's dogma is no longer a stumbling block for the modern reader but a resistance that brings about the poetic energy which we can all appreciate.

The pursuit of one theme throughout five poems as famous as these must necessarily leave out a great deal. This book makes no claim to say everything about the poems that would interest a modern reader. But it is hoped that in trying to show how the moral attitudes are made part of a dramatic experience, I am dealing with a subject that is of interest to all readers of Milton. At the same time I also hope that this book will contribute to the efforts of those critics and aestheticians who are trying to define more precisely the distinctive nature of literature.

It is a pleasure to acknowledge my thanks for personal encouragement to such eminent scholars as the late James H. Hanford, Merritt Y. Hughes, Marjorie H. Nicolson, and to my colleague, Don M. Wolfe. I wish also to acknowledge the help given to me by Paul E. Memmo, Jr., of Fordham University, and my late colleague Richard H. Barker, who have read and commented on the early articles that provided the basis for this book.

I wish to thank the editors of the following journals for

accepting and allowing me to reprint the following articles: *Milton Studies* for "Milton's *Ode* and the Pagan Deities" (1970); *College English* for "Milton's *Samson* and the Modern Reader" (October 1966) and "Poetry and Dogma in *Paradise Lost,* Book VIII" (April 1968), *PMLA* for "The Reader in *Paradise Regained*" (May 1970); *Tennessee Studies in Literature* for "The Unwilling Martyrdom of *Samson Agonistes*" (1968).

My thanks are also extended to Joan Hays who typed the first draft and to Adrienne Bankoff who typed the final draft of the manuscript.

All of the quotations from the poetry, as well as the translations from the Latin poetry are taken from the Douglas Bush edition of *The Complete Poetical Works of John Milton* (Boston, 1965). The quotations from Milton's prose are taken from Merritt Y. Hughes' edition of *Milton, Prose Selections* (New York, 1947).

Lawrence W. Hyman

THE QUARREL WITHIN

I

Milton's Beliefs
and Contextualist Criticism

THE LAST TWO decades has seen great progress in the attempt
to break down the traditional distinction between form and
content in Milton's poetry. By examining Milton's use of symbol, metaphor, and myth, as well as the patterns of imagery, the
critics have enabled us to see Milton's language as more than a
medium through which noble ideas and feelings are expressed;
the language can now be seen as a shaping force in the very
creation of these ideas and feelings. Instead of thinking of the
poems as being created out of the ideas and feelings of the poet,
we can, to some extent, think of the ideas and feelings as being
created out of the poetry.

Only a few critics have gone so far; and I would not assert
that contextualist criticism has caught up with Milton to the
same extent as it has with other poets. But to the extent that
contextualist critics have made us aware of the significance of
Milton's language, they have also enabled us to go beyond a
simple response to Milton's doctrines. In my own attempt to
show how the doctrinal significance of the major poems is transformed by the poetry, I am indebted to these critics, as my
references will make clear. But the scope as well as the purpose
of this book will be made clearer by a brief note on what has
already been accomplished.

In their edition of the *Poems of Mr. John Milton* (1951),
Cleanth Brooks and J. E. Hardy were the first to offer a contextualist reading of the poems written before 1645. There is an
emphasis on the ambivalence of Milton's religious feelings and

3

an attempt to show how this ambivalence is manifested in the language of the poems. Instead of becoming a problem, as they were to traditional and didactic critics, the ambivalence and the paradoxes are seen by Brooks and Hardy as a source of a complexity in feeling that enriches the poems. Frank Kermode in *The Living Milton* (1961) collected a series of essays on all of Milton's major poems with a similar purpose; that is, to read Milton as one reads any poet, and not to be distracted by the value and seriousness of his ideas apart from their poetic context. These individual critics, naturally enough, employ various means of accomplishing this purpose; but the effect of most of their essays is part of a general tendency to find the value of the poems apart from our agreement or disagreement with the doctrines embedded in them.

But the major development in Milton criticism in the last two decades is concerned even more directly with language. The pioneer study is Rosemond Tuve's *Images and Themes in Five Poems by Milton* (1954), and the most successful is Isabel MacCaffrey's *Paradise Lost as Myth* (1959). Despite Miss Tuve's explicit disavowal of contextualism, I would place her work in this tradition because she too is concerned with language not as a mere craft, a technical accompaniment of religious feelings, but as shaping force in the creation of these feelings. The diction, the metaphors, the rhythmic patterns of the poems, as interpreted by Rosemond Tuve, Isabel MacCaffrey, Jackson Cope, and others, are seen not as aspects of *form*, in the traditional sense of that word, but as essential elements in the total imaginative experience. The formal elements are considered, not as mere vehicles for expressing ideas and feelings that Milton had already expressed in his prose, but as elements that shape these feelings and ideas. *Paradise Lost,* for Mrs. MacCaffrey, "is not an argument but the presentation of a single interconnected universe, where the vehicle and the tenor are one." [1]

Such investigations into Milton's language do not *in themselves* support the tendency to shift our perspective away from the didactic interpretations of the poetry. In fact, one scholar has used the distinction between metaphoric and allegorical language to support her belief that the reader in *Paradise Lost* should accept unquestioningly the orthodox attitude expressed by the narrator.[2] But whatever the intention of the critic, his success in focusing our attention on the mythic, metaphoric, or symbolic qualities of language is bound to result in an emphasis on the ambivalence and paradox of a work. For it is the nature of myth, metaphor, and symbol to bring together those forces and ideas that are contrary and disassociated in discursive language. Once we assume that the vehicle and the tenor, the image and the conceptual meaning embodied in the image, are one, we find it difficult to establish a conceptual meaning that points in a particular direction. Once we take into account all of the implications of the concrete images and actions, we are likely to find meanings that go beyond our conceptual categories.

To find such meanings does not, however, imply that we are further removed, or that we are placing the poetic experience away from the ideas and values of everyday experience. The *autonomy* of a literary work, if that term is to continue to be a useful one, must be distinguished from the autonomy of a musical composition. Unlike the notes in music, words, whatever else they may do, still refer to the recognizable objects and ideas in our ordinary life. The values in a poem are also the values that we talk about outside of the poem. The pride of Satan or the humility of Adam, or the despair of Samson, or the death of Lycidas are identical with the pride, humility, despair, and death that we know in the real world. But these familiar and easily recognizable concepts and feelings take on different meanings in the context of the individual poems; our conventional feelings towards these concepts are changed. And it is this change, this difference, that is significant for the literary critic. For the difference, or the uniqueness of Satan's pride and Samson's despair is a product of the language and the structure of the poems. The form determines the significance of the content. Or, to put it another way, it is only from the outside that the ideas and feelings in literature can be considered as *content*. Within the poem, as one critic has aptly stated, there is no dichotomy: "Form is what *goes on in* the poem: The poem as form is the poem in itself."[3]

The emphasis, therefore, on the internal relationship of the elements of Milton's poems should not result in any neglect of the profound religious feelings and argumentative subtleties that enter into the poems. What should be clear, however, is the great change that occurs when abstract ideas and simple feelings are made part of a complex artistic structure. What this change involves, speaking in general terms, is that the definite moral convictions and simple feelings become as complex as the language and the structure into which they are embodied. Instead of a simple opposition between faith and doubt, obedience to God and obedience to one's emotions, hope and despair, we have complex feelings in which contradictory ideas and opposing impulses are both present. Of course many critics and ordinary readers have seen these contradictions in Milton, particularly in *Paradise Lost*. To those readers who are interested in the ideas outside of the poetic context, the contradictions present problems. To the contextualist, however, these contradictions are seen as the inevitable result of the process by which content becomes form. Instead of problems that have to be solved, I will consider the contradictory feelings as the emotional center that gives the poem its dramatic intensity.

My chief objection to the work of the more traditional Miltonists is their failure to distinguish the religious feelings and ideas that are part of Milton's intellectual background, and that are often found in his prose pamphlets, from these feelings *after* they are made part of a dramatic context. Many critics regard the ideas or the religious values in themselves as the chief end of the poetry. In doing so, they fail to realize that the total emotional experience of the entire poem may be quite different from the idea or moral principle that went into the poem. The literary critic, as distinguished from the moralist, should not be concerned with the ability of the poem to reinforce some religious truth, but with the poetic experience. He should, as T. S. Eliot said, try to find out "what was *not* in existence before the poem was completed."[4] (The emphasis is mine.)

A good example of the failure to distinguish the moral doctrine from the poetic experience can be seen in a recent criticism of *Paradise Lost*. In *Surprised By Sin*, Stanley Fish accepts the fact that most readers are sympathetic to the sinful actions of Satan and of Adam. And unlike many of the traditional Miltonists, he does not try to argue us out of such feelings. But this sympathy for sinful actions, Mr. Fish maintains, is only a means whereby we are made aware of our own sinful natures. Like Adam, the reader is meant to fall into sin and by means of self-knowledge and contrition to achieve grace. The entire poem is, according to this critic, a religious experience by which the reader "is brought first to self-knowledge and then to contrition, and finally perhaps, to grace and everlasting bliss."[5]

My own interpretation of the poem will be given in the appropriate chapter. What concerns us here are not the specific comments but the assumption that reading *Paradise Lost* is similar to a religious experience. Milton himself, of course, felt very strongly that poetry could lead to virtuous actions, that it could serve "beside the office of a pulpit, to inbreed and cherish in a great people the seeds of virtue and public civility. . . ."[6] And Stanley Fish, in common with a number of other Miltonists, cites these opinions concerning the function of poetry to support his statement that "Milton's concern with the ethical imperatives of political and social behaviour would hardly allow him to write an epic which did not attempt to give his audience a basis for moral action."[7]

Enough has been said about the intentional fallacy during the last two decades to preclude any need to pursue the question of how to determine the true intention of a writer. A recent attempt to revive the concept of the author's intention as a means of achieving greater objectivity in interpreting a poem has not been very successful.[8] But aside from the general theory, no one can deny that any interpretation of a poem must rest on the evidence found in the poem itself. For it is not the poem that Milton intended to write, but the poem that he actually did write that confronts the reader. Of course, the poems themselves do show, quite explicitly at times, that Milton was trying "to give his audience a basis for moral action." And my own readings will try to account for these statements. But once we go to the text for evidence, we must also be prepared to find evidence that goes beyond the artist's intentions. For the poems of Milton, like all works of art, have an existence of their own. They would not be works of art if they were only expressions of ideas and feelings that have significance only to their creator. Like paintings and songs, literary works have different meanings, not only for different eras, but for different readers. No attempt at critical objectivity can escape the fact that what we see in a poem, as in any object, is determined not only by the poem but by the presuppositions and the expectations of the readers at a given time. As Murray Krieger has pointed out, "the *a priori* are in control, constituting what they see by limiting how they see it . . . the perspective that determines what we would have the work be in order to make sense of its parts is in turn determined by our prior notion, implicit or explicit of what we will value in poetry—or value as poetry."[9]

Such an admission of the limits to objectivity does not imply that all interpretations are impressionistic, and that there can be no reasoned argument in favor of one as against another. There are, obviously, standard meanings in the words and sentences of any poem or novel, and no good critic can fail to take these standard meanings into account. Furthermore, there can be, and often is during the same generation, a similarity in the values that we find in good poetry, or in what we value as poetry. My own preconceptions, what I am looking for in the poetry of Milton, are, I believe, similar to those of many contemporary readers. And although these assumptions will be implicit throughout the book, it will be helpful for the reader to have them made explicit. For it is this view of what poetry can do, in contrast to philosophy and religion, that marks the chief difference between this book and the dominant trend in present day criticism of Milton, at least in this country.

That literature has a function which is fundamentally different from that of philosophy or religion is based on the assumption that the literary experience is different from the experience we encounter in everyday life. This view of literature has a long history. But a recent writer, Dorothy Walsh, has expressed it most succinctly: "The experience incarnated in the poem, the experience that is the very substance of the poem, is not actual experience. It cannot be said to be the poet's experience, since the poet is a person and any experience of a person is a perishing occurrence. . . . As something 'made', rather than merely found, it cannot only be shaped and formed by the literary artist, but elaborated and developed in point of subtlety and in point of complexity."[10] Such an assumption does not imply that there is no continuity between the imaginative experience that we will find in the epics, lyrics, and dramatic poems of Milton and the religious experience of Milton himself. But to distinguish between the poetic experience and the actual experience does allow us to find in the poems a significance that is qualitatively different from the experience that Milton might have had. "As something 'made', rather than merely found," Milton's poems can be expected to possess a subtlety and a complexity that goes beyond the "contrition," the "grace," and the "everlasting bliss" that Stanley Fish and other critics find. And it is in search of such a complexity, in our moral response as well as in our response to the language, that the following essays are presented.

NOTES

1. Isabel MacCaffrey, *Paradise Lost as "Myth"* (Cambridge, Mass., 1959), p. 108.
2. Anne Ferry, *The Narrator in Paradise Lost* (Cambridge, Mass., 1963).
3. Duncan Robertson, "The Dichotomy of Form and Content." *College English* 28 (January 1967), 297.
4. *The Use of Poetry and the Use of Criticism* (New York, 1933), p. 138.
5. Stanley Fish, *Surprised By Sin, The Reader in Paradise Lost* (New York, 1967), p. 38.
6. *The Reason of Church Government Urged Against Prelaty in John Milton, Prose Selections,* Book II, ed. Merritt Y. Hughes (New York, 1947), p. 107.
7. Fish, op. cit., p. 1.
8. E. D. Hirsh, *Validity in Interpretation* (New Haven, Conn., 1967). Mr. Hirsh's argument has been refuted, I believe, by a number of critics. See *Genre* I (July 1968), 3; and *Contemporary Literature* (Summer 1968), 9,3.
9. *Contemporary Literature* (Summer 1968), 292.
10. *Literature and Knowledge* (Middletown, Conn., 1969), p. 90.

II

The *Nativity Ode* and the Pagan Deities

ABOUT THE TIME that he had completed or was completing the hymn *On the Morning of Christ's Nativity* (often referred to as the *Nativity Ode*), the 21-year-old Milton commented upon it to his friend Charles Diodati:

> Now if you would like to know what I am doing . . . I am singing the prince of peace, the son of Heaven, and the blessed ages promised in the sacred books—the cries of the infant God, and the lodgment in a poor stable of him who with his Father rules the realms above; I am singing of the starry sky and the hymns of the angelic host in the upper air, and the pagan gods suddenly destroyed at their own shrines.

This sentence, translated from Milton's Latin poem *Elegia Sexta,* gives us a fair outline of the argument in the *Ode,* as well as an indication of the heightened feelings of a young man who has just written his first great poem. But the entire elegy, or verse letter, in which this sentence appears gives us a clue to another aspect of the *Ode,* one which has stimulated a great deal of comment on the part of Milton scholars: the banishment of the pagan gods. Why should a poem on the nativity end with the vision of "the pagan gods suddenly destroyed at their own shrines"? Would it not be more appropriate for such a poem to conclude on an affirmative note, such as "the hymns of the angelic host"?

I agree with most readers that the negative feelings associated with these banished deities does not in any way disturb the dominant mood of the poem. No one seems to be troubled by

10

the apparent shift in emphasis from the infant Christ in the first part of the poem to the pagan gods in the concluding section. Milton has undoubtedly succeeded in maintaining a unified mood throughout. But to understand and appreciate this unity we should, I believe, recognize an ambivalence in Milton's attitude towards Christianity, particularly towards the Incarnation. To Milton, in this poem at least, the birth of Christ brings about a sense of loss as well as a sense of triumph; and the ambivalent attitude towards the pagan deities is therefore an extension of the attitude towards the Nativity itself. The departure of the pagan gods is linked more closely with the first part of the poem than we would assume. The sense of loss that is associated with the false gods can be seen even in the coming of the true God.

For sixteen of its thirty-two stanzas, the movement of the poem is a steady one. We go from the "rude manger" covered with snow to the "globe of circular light," which breaks forth into a celestial music of "such holy song" as will make us believe that "Time will run back and fetch the age of gold." The movement is forward and upward, literally, that is geographically, as well as emotionally, until we feel that heaven itself "Will open wide the gates of her high palace hall." But we are then quickly reminded that we are anticipating, that the second coming, the return of the golden age, although implicit in the coming of the infant Christ, will actually occur only at the end of time. The immediate effect of the Nativity is the destruction of Satan's kingdom on earth. Or rather, the beginning of that destruction, since it will be completed only at the last judgment. But it is the beginning of that destruction that the poet is interested in. After a brief reference to the day of judgment, stanzas 19–25 are devoted to the immediate manifestation of the destruction of Satan's kingdom: the disappearance of the pagan gods.

The oracles are silenced; Apollo, Peor, Ashtoreth, Moloch, Isis and Osiris are banished, or at least no longer appear at their usual haunts, while "With flow'r-inwoven tresses torn/The nymphs in twilight shade of tangled thickets mourn." The gods are banished with such lovely images and such gentle sorrow that many readers have wondered whether the poet himself is also mourning for the loss of these gods and goddesses of the classical world. Why, some critics have asked, does the poet celebrate the coming of Christ by dwelling, particularly in the closing movement of the poem, on such a beautiful aspect of the pagan world:

> The lonely mountains o'er
> And the resounding shore.
>   A voice of weeping heard and loud lament;
> From haunted spring and dale
> Edged with poplar pale
>   The parting Genius is with sighing sent;
> With flow'r-inwoven tresses torn
> The nymphs in twilight shade of tangled thickets mourn.

This banishment of the classical deities who haunt the springs, dales, mountains, and shores, has an obvious relationship to Milton's own decision to turn away from classical poetry, much as he admired it, in order to become a Christian poet. As he said some years later, in *The Reason of Church Government*, he wished to write poetry that had the "power, beside the office of a pulpit, to inbreed and cherish in a great people the seeds of virtue and public civility, to allay the perturbations of the mind and set the affections in right tune."[1] The biographical critics, most notably James Hanford, Arthur Barker, and A. S. P. Woodhouse, have therefore related this passage in the *Ode* to important decisions in Milton's own life. Woodhouse points out how much Milton rejoices in the pagan deities in the *Elegia Quinta;* yet is ready to banish them in the *Ode* "because he (Milton) is ready to accept the supremacy of the order of grace over nature herself."[2] Arthur Barker, also relating the conflict in the poem to a similar conflict in Milton's early life, finds that the poem transcends "the conflict between the two traditions" to bring about a "harmonious perfection symbolized by the music of the spheres."[3]

Critics who tend to look more closely at the text than at Milton's life have also tried to reconcile the heavenly light and heavenly music that dominates the first half of the poem with the plaintive tone and the dark shadows of the second half. Rosemond Tuve, who offers us the most thorough analysis of the imagery, denies that there is any conflict between the pagan and the Christian elements in the poem. "It is not the war between these two principles to which we must attend, but the seed of a peace between them in that the Light, being love, took on the Darkness to bring it back to His own nature:

> That glorious Form, that Light unsufferable
> And that far-beaming blaze of Majesty,
> . . . .
> He laid aside; and here with us to be,
>   Forsook the Courts of everlasting Day,
> And chose with us a darksome House of mortal Clay."[4]

The "peace" which Miss Tuve finds in the poem is between the Light brought by Christ and the light of Nature; for Nature, however sinful it may be, is redeemable. With the pagan deities, however, Miss Tuve has more difficulty. She at first is willing to admit that they must be banished because, unlike Nature, "they do not acknowledge" their "inferiority" to Christ. But she soon realizes that the banishment of the deities might bring her up against the old problem, and she is determined not to "be caught into thinking that Milton stood on the brink of a Puritanical antipathy, to become worse later; toward pagan thought—nymphs, fays, Apollo and the rest."[5] We are told that Milton could accept the beauty of these nymphs and fays as long as they were not worshipped as gods. We can thus banish the "sacredness" of these gods without at the same time banishing their loveliness.

But realizing, perhaps, that if these gods are banished they are banished as indivisible entities with their true "loveliness" as well as their false "sacredness," Miss Tuve proceeds to distinguish between Satan (or Leviathan in this poem) who deceived us into worshipping the false gods and the gods themselves, and between some of the gods who reveal the loveliness of truth and others who "are vicious and savage." The further we go into these subtle discriminations the further we get from the poem, and also from Miss Tuve's determination to deny any conflict between Milton's Christianity and his love for the pagan gods.[6] It would be much simpler to admit that there is a conflict inherent in any action that banishes a world that we also find beautiful. And there is nothing to detract from Milton's greatness as a poet, or as a man, in allowing him to express this conflict. We should not, as critics of Milton's poetry, be concerned with Miss Tuve's desire (shared by a number of critics) to keep Milton firmly within a medieval tradition of untroubled Christian orthodoxy.

What is justified, however, in Miss Tuve's intentions, is her desire to see the poem as a unified composition. For most readers feel this unity as they read the poem—rather than a tension between pagan and Christian sympathies. But the unity in the poem is a different matter from the unity in Milton's own conception of how a love of the classical past can be made logically consistent with a rather Hebraic concept of Christianity. The unity of the poetic experience does not depend on a logically coherent compromise between contrary attitudes. On the contrary, the unity in art is richer and more interesting when it can accept attitudes and beliefs that are contradictory in everyday experience. Contradictions have to be resolved when we have to act, or to "take a stand" one way or the other. But in art we do not take a stand; instead we are concerned with exploring the complex interrelationship of our feelings, particularly those feelings that move in different directions.

Some sense of such a unity is described by Cleanth Brooks and J. E. Hardy, who find that Milton "does not emphasize this element [the contrast between the two halves of the poem] to the point of making a contradiction between such regret and the great joy caused by Christ's birth. The tone of the poem is too simple to admit of such tensions." And this lack of tension is explained by a kind of aesthetic distance. "We are never close up to the scene. This sense of distance and detachment is achieved in part by the cosmic sweep of the Hymn."[7] Brooks and Hardy are right, I believe, in looking for the unity within the poem, in the way that the poem is composed, rather than in a logical coherence between the conflicting feelings. And there is undoubtedly some truth in their remark about the "sense of distance and detachment" that Milton is able to achieve in his depiction of both the coming of Christ and the disappearance of the classical gods and goddesses. But this sense of detachment must not be so interpreted as to indicate that Milton is not

deeply involved in both the celestial music that announces the
Nativity:

> Ring out, ye crystal spheres
> Once bless our human ears
> . . . .
> And let the bass of heaven's deep organ blow

and the desolation that is felt at the disappearance of the old
gods:

> In consecrated earth
> and on the holy hearth
>   The Lars and Lemures moan with midnight plaint.

If we do use the word "detachment" we must be careful to
distinguish the "detachment" of poetry from the meaning of
this word in ordinary experience. But the unified tone of the
poem can be explained more simply and directly by looking
again at the imagery. Despite the excellent analyses of the
language by the previously mentioned critics (as well as by
others) it has not yet been pointed out that the departure of the
deities is emotionally related to the advent of Christ. For
regret and joy experienced simultaneously, so that one feeling
cannot be separated from the other, is inherent in the paradox
of the Christian myth. In this poem the coming of Christ brings
pain and death as a necessary prelude to joy and eternal life.
Miss Tuve has already pointed out that the Light (in the
second stanza), the image that is most closely related to divinity, is brought to earth in "a darksome house of mortal clay."
This paradox is continued in the "Hymn" itself by the emphasis
on "winter," "midnight," and the cold snow, all of which
prevent the sun from giving life to the earth. The bringer of
eternal life comes to mankind in a scene that seems to deny all
life. The "universal peace" that follows represents, it is true, the
final victory *over* death. But at this point even this "peace"
is presented by the absence of all sound, which seems to be in
contrast to the celestial harmony that it suggests. The silence is
in contrast to the heavenly music just as the darkness is in
contrast to the celestial light. Of course we realize that "The

Sun himself withheld his wonted speed" because "He saw a greater Sun appear/Than his bright throne and burning axle-tree could bear." But we are not to forget the darkness that is the immediate result of the advent of the Prince of Light.

Thus the paradox inherent in the Christian story—the fact that the power and the glory of heaven is brought to us by an infant who, in contrast to the "angelic symphony" cannot even speak, and who in contrast to the celestial light is surrounded with darkness—prepares us for the final section of the poem. For at this point we are told that the advent of God who has come to redeem the earth and its inhabitants brings about, as its very first consequence, the disappearance of those gods who for thousands of years infused nature with divinity. And it is precisely this, the power to unify nature and man, that Christ seems to lack.

It may seem strange to say that the Christ who is sent to redeem man and nature from original sin cannot infuse nature with the divinity that was given by the gods, nymphs, and fauns who inhabited the streams and woods of pagan myths. Certainly Christ's incarnation is a symbol of the redemption of nature as well as of man. But Milton, as a number of scholars have already seen, was never able to accept the Incarnation completely. According to Malcolm M. Ross, "Milton was unable to imagine poetically the humanity of God. His symbolization of Christ is never incarnational." And because Milton could never fully accept a vision of the world in which the natural world was joined to Christ, he needed these pagan deities in the *Nativity Ode*. "By an ingenious process of reversal," Ross continues, "the sensuous value of heathen legend is brought in through the back door to add poetic 'body' to the positive but chaste images of light, and order—yet never to merge with them. . . ."[8]

I would disagree with the phrase "the back door" as well as with Mr. Ross' contention that the sensuous beauty fails to merge with the heavenly sound and "light unsufferable." It seems to me that the beauty of the pagan deities is not *meant* to merge with the beauty of the Christian heaven. That is why those deities are banished. The disappearance of the pagan gods is thus made continuous with the first part of the poem. For Milton reminds us that the glory and joy that Christ will bring must come about through His suffering on the Cross, and that the celestial harmony will be ushered in by the Last Judgment when

> The aged Earth, aghast
> With terror at the blast,
>   Shall from the surface to the center shake.

If the Prince of Peace must be crucified by the hatred of men and the celestial harmony brought in with a terrifying "blast," we are prepared for the fact that the divinity that shall one day bathe all earth in a heavenly light must first banish those gods who have heretofore allowed man to feel at one with nature.

The regret that we feel at the departure of the divinities is therefore a genuine regret. The loss of the old divinities as a prelude to the coming of the true Divinity is comparable to the contrast between the rude manger in which Christ appears and the kingdom of earth and heaven that he will inherit. When we know what will occur as a result of the immediate action, when we know that this cold dark night will usher in a greater light than the Sun could ever give, our attitude towards the immediate scene is changed. But not completely; for we do not erase the immediate sensation of darkness or of helplessness or of pain. The "bitter grief" that we feel at the crucifixion is part of the joy that we feel at the eventual triumph over death. The ecstasy of the Christian is made up of both the pain and the triumph. It is not the negation of one feeling by a contrasting feeling but the fusion of both that creates the distinctive quality of Christian ecstasy.

Once these contrasts in the advent of Christ are recognized, we can see that there is no real change in mood when we are told that the first step in bringing about an age of gold is the removal of the pagan gods. We know that in the future

> Truth and Justice then
> Will down return to men,
>   Orbed in a rainbow; and like glories weaving
> Mercy will sit between,
> Throned in celestial sheen,
>   With radiant feet the tissued clouds down steering.

But such knowledge does not negate the sense of loss that we feel at the present moment, when we no longer have the presence of any gods to bring us close to the natural world:

Nor is Osiris seen
In Memphian grove or green,
    Trampling the unshow'red grass with lowings loud;
Nor can he be at rest
Within his sacred chest
    Naught but profoundest hell can be his shroud;
In vain with timbreled anthems dark
The sable-stoled sorcerers bear his worshipped ark.

The similarity between the feelings towards the coming of Christ and the departure of the false gods is strengthened by these images of darkness. Just as the Prince of Light came to us in the darkness of winter only to bring about a greater light, so He, the Prince of Light, now inaugurates a heaven on earth by causing Osiris, the god of green groves, to disappear into "profoundest hell." Everything that is good, everything that reaches to the light of heaven, is first brought into the poem by what is cold and dark here below. Even the music of the spheres has as its prologue the "timbreled anthems dark;" while in the following stanza the celestial brightness brings about darkness: "The rays of Bethlehem *blind* [the] dusky eyn" of another pagan god. The paradox of the infant who becomes king, of the darkness that brings light, thus permeates the entire poem, and allows us to feel as well as to see that aspect of Christianity that brings us to ecstatic joy by means of loss and suffering.

It is not only by imagery but, more subtly and more strikingly, by his use of time that Milton enables us to experience, simultaneously, the immediate sense of the action and its future significance. As a number of critics have already noted, the poem constantly brings together the future and the past within the present moment. "Indeed the Christian ideas of the circularity of time and the simultaneity of all moments under the aspect of eternity underlie the inmost structure of the poem."⁹ We are in the presence of the young poet on Christmas morning in 1629, at the nativity 1629 years earlier, and with the quiring angels as they bring in a new heaven and a new earth at the moment when time comes to an end. For this reason we are emotionally able to experience the painful effect of the birth, the crucifixion, and the last judgment at the same time as we experience the ecstatic joy of the marriage of heaven and earth. By allowing us to experience the future and the past in the present moment, the poem also allows us to experience the contrary emotions that are associated with the different events simultaneously. Everything comes together at the moment of Christ's birth; it is "a moment of astonishment."[10]

The harmony that pervades this poem is, therefore, not the result of the Christian attitude overcoming the love for the classical gods, or the result of some logical reconciliation between Milton's regret at the departure of these gods and his Christian faith. The beliefs and feelings that Milton had as a man certainly go into the poem; but their function is not to convince us of anything but to allow us to see how contrary feelings brought to the surface by the Nativity can be reconciled into a harmony. And the harmony, as I have tried to show, is not brought about by the objectivity of an essayist or an historian who allows us to see what is good or bad in both the Christian and the non-Christian beliefs. It is the objectivity brought about by a poet who can fuse both a sense of loss and a sense of triumph into the imagery and structure of the poem.

We are thus unable to answer the old questions as to whether Milton, at the time he wrote the poem, is turning away from the pagan spirit, or whether he is doing so with regret or with untroubled joy. For although these personal feelings enter into the poem, the feelings created by the poem are something else, and go beyond any personal belief on the part of the poet or the reader. There is nothing *in* the poem to agree or disagree with. The beliefs are used by Milton to show the complex emotions that they can bring forth. We are not asked, therefore, to move in any particular direction—to rejoice or to mourn for the loss of the pagan gods—but simply to join the poet in a growing awareness of how contradictory feelings are brought into a harmony. And this harmony is brought about by the power of poetry to make us experience diverse events simultaneously. Fortunately, such harmony, unlike that described in the poem, can be heard by mortal ears.

NOTES

1. *The Reason of Church Government Urged Against Prelaty* in *John Milton, Prose Selections,* Book II, ed. Merritt Y. Hughes (New York, 1947), p. 107.

2. "Notes on Milton's Early Development," *UTQ* XIII (1943), 77.

3. "The Patterns of Milton's *Nativity Ode,*" *UTQ* X (1941), 180.

4. *Images and Themes in Five Poems by Milton* (Cambridge, Mass., 1957), p. 47.

5. Ibid., p. 64.

6. To prove, as Miss Tuve has attempted, that the love of pagan gods, or a certain respectful regard for them, is consistent with the doctrines of such early Christians as Lactantius and Prudentius, is beside the point. Readers find the conflicting attitudes towards these gods in the poem, and in Milton's other works. The fact that some Christians could easily accept the pagan gods does not mean that all could do so. In any case, it is impossible to argue that Milton's Christian beliefs were always the same as those of the Church fathers. See Malcolm M. Ross, note 8 below.

7. *Poems of Mr. John Milton* (New York, 1951), p. 103.

8. *Poetry and Dogma* (New Brunswick, N.J., 1954), pp. 188, 194.

9. Lowry Nelson, Jr., *Baroque Lyric Poetry* (New Haven, Conn., 1961), p. 51.

10. Laurence Stapleton, "Milton and the New Music," *UTQ* XXIII (1953–54), 226. (Mr. Stapleton takes the phrase from Paul Valéry.)

III

Lycidas and the Problem of Belief

FEW POEMS IN our language have received so much praise as
Lycidas. And despite the claim made by M. H. Abrams in his
excellent essay, "Five Types of *Lycidas*," the poem that we
admire and interpret in so many ways is essentially the same
poem.[1] Different readers and different critical approaches do
indeed, as Professor Abrams points out, emphasize different
aspects of the poem, but there is no basic disagreement concerning the main theme, or the progression of thought and feeling.
However we may describe the loss suffered by the speaker in
the poem, the "uncouth swain," we can all accept that his loss of
faith in a world order that allows death to strike a young
man is eventually overcome by the belief in immortality. Whatever doubts the speaker has about the value of his own efforts,
the value of poetry in general, and the justice of God's ways are
certainly resolved in the triumphal conclusion in which

> Lycidas, sunk low, but mounted high
> Through the dear might of him that walked the waves,
> . . . .
> . . . hears the unexpressive nuptial song
> In the blest kingdoms meek of joy and love.

We can go further, I believe, and say that few readers and
critics have been troubled by this conclusion, even when they
themselves lack any strong convictions about immortality. Our
appreciation of this poem is not dependent on any belief in
immortality or in any scheme, Christian or pagan, which finds a
just and rational order behind or above the visible world of

21

contingency. Nor is there anything in the poem itself that would give us any logical basis for reaching the conclusion of the speaker. The fact that the sun rises in the east after setting in the west is no reason for concluding that the dead Lycidas will someday become immortal. The resurrection of Lycidas "In the blest kingdoms meek of joy and love," is accepted by the speaker of the poem as a matter of faith, not of logic. The absence of a logical development in the argument does not seem to interfere with our appreciation of the poem. It is obvious that our participation in "the unexpressive nuptial song" while reading the poem is quite different from our acceptance of a doctrine of immortality outside of the poem.

But what is not so obvious is just how we can distinguish the poetic experience from a religious experience, or from a philosophical commitment, without trivializing the poem—that is, without reading the poem only for its beautiful patterns of sound and imagery. It is a difficult task, and one which can easily lead us away from the poem into an abstruse discussion of aesthetics. But to neglect this task is to give the impression, often by indirection, that our complete response to *Lycidas* is dependent on our acceptance, in some way, of a belief in immortality, or in a related doctrine that would coincide with the religious consolation offered by the poem. For example, in a recent essay devoted primarily to the patterns of rhyme in *Lycidas*, the author asserts that *"Lycidas'* form, then, reveals what the poem is about. It insists emphatically that order lies beneath apparent chaos and is perceived in all its glory by the eye that probes beneath the surface into the heart of things."[2] Nothing is said here about the reader's belief in this order; and by this failure to distinguish the religious from the poetic experience, Professor Wittreich leaves open the possibility that the two are the same, and consequently that in appreciating *Lycidas* we are undergoing a religious experience.

Of course, a number of critics have tried to make clear the difference between the doctrine within the poem and the doctrine *per se*, and I will refer to some of them in passing. I intend to go somewhat further, however, and try to show that our disbelief in the doctrines embodied in the poem is assumed by the poet, and that it is the poem itself that provides the basis for the dualism in our response. It is the pastoral tradition, particularly as this tradition is given renewed power by Milton's deliberate and highly conscious control over his form, not our twentieth-century scepticism, that makes us see the resurrection in *Lycidas* as an aesthetic experience rather than as a religious belief. The formal structure is by no means submerged in the emotional "content" of the poem; for the most obvious characteristic of the poem is the self-conscious way in which the poet calls attention to his form. We are not allowed to forget that whatever the emotion may be, we are reading or listening to a pastoral elegy. And it' is this emphasis on the formal structure that enables us to separate or distance our feelings about immortality as a doctrine from our feelings about the immortality that becomes part of the poem.

But before showing exactly how this separation between poetry and doctrine is accomplished, it will be helpful to see what happens to our reading of the poem when no provision is made for the distancing effects of the formal elements. My first example is from an essay by Jon S. Lawry. According to this interpretation, the grief suffered by the speaker of the poem is not caused by the loss of Edward King, or Lycidas, but by the speaker's loss of faith in the power of poetry to confront the harsh reality of death. "Melodious artistic lament—the essential concern of which is neither King nor Milton but the expression itself within the formal determinations of the genre—is confronted by the anguished recognition of real physical loss, of defected promise, and of corrupt society. Lament veers sharply away from the provinces of 'pure art' as the vulnerable poet himself and his equally vulnerable creations become its subject." And this critic goes on to show the "progressive surrender of the pastoral attitude," as the harsh reality of Edward King's death continually reasserts itself. Poetry proves incapable of overcoming the pain of Lycidas' death; only Christian immortality can do so. For "pastoral poetry in and of itself is weak before the onslaught of actuality, but actuality itself gradually has been discovered to rest within a vastly larger aspect, that of eternity. . . . Lycidas in his way becomes transformed from victim to saviour, like Christ; he is delivered beyond the lament of either pastoral or reality."[3]

Most readers would not be satisfied, I believe, with the sharp distinction made by Mr. Lawry between the pastoral-pagan tradition and the Christian. The intermingling of pagan and Christian allusions and the assumption that pagan myths prefigured Christian truths, have been emphasized by many scholars. As Marjorie Nicolson has mentioned, Jove and Orpheus become God and Christ so imperceptibly that "Pagan and Christian, death and life, the two strains combine in the triumphal conclusion in which they are inextricably conjoined."[4] But there is no denying Mr. Lawry's statement that poetry is incapable of saving Lycidas from death, or of overcoming the poet's grief over that death. The nymphs, even had they been present, could have done nothing, we are told, to save Lycidas; nor could the Muse herself prevent the destruction of Orpheus, "her inchanting son." But it is just as certain that no one expects poetry to have this kind of power. Milton is not writing in such a way as to affect the everyday world of action. We are constantly made aware of the fact that pastoral elegy is its own world, and that this world is created by the poets who work, or sing, in that tradition. Lycidas is quite consciously a fiction; but of course a "necessary fiction," to use Wallace Stevens' term.

That Milton refers to the primitive, magical power of poetry may represent a desire that words alone might have an effect on actual experience. Or it might be merely another way of rooting his poem in a primitive conception of word magic in order to strengthen or reinforce the naïveté that is part of the pastoral mood. But in any case we can assume that Milton no more expected that poetry itself would *literally* remove the grief of the mourners any more than he expected the dolphins to carry the body of Lycidas to shore. On a literal basis, as Dr. Johnson said so eloquently, the poem is a failure.

But of course we do not read the poem literally. We are not looking for real tears. We read the poem, or should read it, as Rosemond Tuve has said, figuratively. *Lycidas* "moves entirely on a metaphorical plane."[5] Miss Tuve proceeds to give us a brilliant analysis of the metaphors and images in the poem, to which all critics of *Lycidas* are indebted. But her essay does not see all the implications of a metaphorical reading. For when she reaches the conclusion of the poem, we find no distinction between the figurative use of the resurrection and our literal belief in the inevitable triumph of life over death. "Pastoral has its ways of reasserting a fundamental and harmonious sympathy, and of proclaiming that not decay and death but life and creativity and love is the universal principle, one which is seen (especially, but not solely, as pastoral was Christianized) as having the strength of a divine intention."[6]

This statement, whatever else it may be, is certainly similar to other statements about immortality; and as such, we cannot distinguish our belief in this "universal principle" from our belief in immortality as a doctrine. Suppose we do not believe that "life and creativity and love" will eventually overcome "decay and death." Would such a lack of belief prevent us from assenting to the conclusion of *Lycidas*? G. L. Fraser's answer to this question deserves consideration.

Fraser starts by emphasizing the continuity in the poem between the pagan and the Christian mythologies, and he argues that we can accept them in the same way. The fact that modern readers "accept his [Milton's] Orpheus so easily makes it simple for us to accept, also, his Christ. We can take it all as a mythology if we like, but as mythology very powerfully organized: and it does release in us as in Milton very powerful emotions."[7] So far there is no difficulty in following Mr. Fraser (except for his failure to distinguish emotions in art from emotions in everyday experience, a point that will be taken up later). But when Mr. Fraser goes on to insist that "the survival, the impact upon ourselves of a poem like *Lycidas* is, surely, a very important part of the evidence we have that 'not decay and death but life and creativity is the universal principle,'" we are confronted with the old question of doctrinal truth of the poem. And we are not given any way out of the dilemma by Fraser's conclusion: "What positivist or naturalist, what linguistic analyst, faced say, with the last stanza of Yeats' 'Among School Children' . . . would burst out with 'Oh, but it's not true'? Art makes its own kind of truth."[8]

Most contemporary readers of *Lycidas* are strongly influenced by positivist, naturalist, and analytic tendencies in modern philosophy. And as a result, some of us are not at all convinced that there is any truth, or even any clear meaning, in the statement that "not decay and death, but life and creativity, is the universal principle." It would be difficult to convince such a large group of readers that their continued enjoyment of the poem is in itself evidence, even partial evidence, for the truth of a statement that they would find incapable of proof, and which some would find meaningless. Or if we leave philosophy for common sense, many readers would maintain that death is as much a universal principle as life. All of us who talk about poetry get into difficulty when we use the word *truth*. It might be better, therefore, for all of us to realize that if poetry makes "its own kind of truth" then we had better not use the word *truth*. If the statement that life and creativity is stronger than decay and death depends for its truth (even in part) on our continuing to read *Lycidas,* then we should not refer to the survival of *Lycidas* as evidence. The word *evidence* certainly connotes some sense of objectivity; and we become confused logically if we argue that the immortality of a man must in some way be true because we appreciate a poem that embodies this belief. I agree with Mr. Fraser that we must go beyond the kind of logical empirical thought proper to science if we are to describe the experience of art. But to go beyond does not, I believe, mean that we must go against it.

The best way of getting around the difficulty of *truth* and *belief* is to recognize that literature, as many critics and aestheticians have been telling us for a long time, does not derive its power from its ability to make statements about the empirical world or from its power to affect the emotions that we have in everyday experience. Even an ordinary sermon delivered at Edward King's funeral could give us stronger *evidence* for believing in the resurrection of the dead than the poem. And by so doing, this sermon or prayer could give the mourners a greater consolation than they could receive from reading *Lycidas*. But no sermon, only a poem, could give us a "melodious tear," and such a tear is not wiped away in the ordinary sense of the word. If there are no real tears in *Lycidas* we should not expect a real consolation, that is, a consolation that would be equivalent to a religious or philosophical acceptance of immortality.

But what do we mean, exactly, when we say that the grief in the poem is not real? The grief described here certainly *refers* to the grief that anyone might have for a real person. If the writer creates his own world, this world should not be thought of as having no resemblance to the world that we know in everyday life. The autonomy of art does not mean that we refuse to recognize the familiar world in a poem or in a painting, but that the artist does not want us to respond to *his* world as we do to events in the real world. And to make clear that we do not respond so, the writer or painter transforms his subject so that we are forced to react differently. Edward King, the young man who actually drowned in 1637, is transformed into Lycidas, and the rivers and flowers and winds into Alpheus and Arethusa, Amaranthus, and Hippotades. And by making this change, Milton is changing the grief that we might actually have felt at the funeral into a grief that we enjoy as we hear it develop through the intricate patterns of rhyme and rhythm. All poems do this to some extent; that is, all poems give form to emotions and so transform them. But few poems do this so deliberately and self-consciously as *Lycidas*:

> Begin then, Sisters of the sacred well
> That from beneath the seat of Jove doth spring,
> Begin, and somewhat loudly sweep the string.

It is not necessary to repeat here or to even try to summarize the various patterns of imagery and sound that have been revealed to us by the various critics. Nor is it necessary to argue that this formal structure, embedded in the pastoral tradition, transmutes the grief into something different from the grief that we feel in ordinary life. As J. H. Hanford pointed out many years ago, "Its grief is not of the kind that cries aloud; it soothes and rests us like calm music."[9] Most readers have accepted this artifice as part of the poem. But this acceptance of artifice, in its best sense of course, has not been applied (except by Cleanth Brooks and J. E. Hardy), to the penultimate section, which consoles us with the description of immortality. Perhaps because this doctrine has, for many, a validity outside of the context of the poem, in contrast to the way we accept the nymphs and river gods, a number of readers have regarded the immortality as standing apart from the poem.

But there is no basis for this differentiation in the poem. The opening lines of this section, which ask us to "Weep no more," do not differ in imagery or viewpoint from the rest of the poem. (It is only in the final eight lines, the coda, that there is an abrupt shift in perspective—as we shall soon see.) The key image in these opening lines of this final section is the "sun" which, after sinking "in the ocean bed"

> . . . tricks his beams, and with new-spangled ore
> Flames in the forehead of the morning sky.

The analogy with Lycidas who, "sunk low, but mounted high," maintains the continuity between nature and man that we have seen throughout the poem. But if we had to depend on a logical relationship between these two events, the sun's rising and Lycidas' resurrection, the poem would have little effect.

As Robert French has recently pointed out, there is an astonishingly sudden leap from the pessimistic scenes in the first two-thirds of the poem in which Lycidas is left to the parching winds and a watery bier to the final section (beginning with line 165) in which we are told, along with the "Shepherds" to "Weep no more . . ./For Lycidas your sorrow is not dead." How do we go so quickly from a scene in which we see the dead man's bones "hurl'd . . ./beyond the stormy Hebrides" (line 156) to the injunction "to weep no more," a few lines later, since Lycidas is "In the blest Kingdoms meek of joy and love"? According to Mr. French the speaker in the poem changes, after line 164, from a natural man who sees death as a final end to a Christian believer who sees natural death as only a prelude to immortality: "If the presentation has been effective, the audience will at line 164 be involved in a mood of despair that the poem creates as Lycidas is abandoned to the waves and winds. At this psychologically advantageous point, when hope has been lost, the poet presses upon his audience the message of Christian revelation; instantly the audience is raised from despair, and hope is again possible."[10]

Mr. French's distinction between the two voices of poet is excellent and does help in clarifying the structure. But the distinction between the two moods within the poem is not as

basic as the distinction between the feelings within the poem
and the feelings that exist outside of the poem. If the reader at
the conclusion of the poem is not "raised from despair" and has
no more faith in immortality than he had before, would we
doubt whether the *poetic* experience "has been effective"? Surely
not. Few readers would give their assent to such a complete
identification between the effectiveness of the doctrine and the
poem.

John Milton, of course, may have believed in the resurrection
of the soul and of the body at this time, but the poet's belief in
immortality was based on much more solid grounds than the
analogy of the rising sun. The belief in immortality for both
Milton and his readers has its origin and its evidence outside of the poem. Within the poem, the miracle of "him who
walked the waves" is simply another metaphor for the resurrection of Lycidas, and is to be accepted in the same way as the
pagan fables of Arethusa and the dolphins. What we assent to
here is precisely what we assented to throughout the poem: the
possibility of imagining a world, or a cosmos, in which man and
nature are intimately related in a rational pattern of growth,
death, and renewal. We feel at the conclusion the completion of
this pattern; and our satisfaction is an aesthetic feeling, not a
religious one.

That we are meant to accept the immortality of Lycidas as
part of an imaginative experience and not as an empirical truth,
can be seen in the final section, in which the poet, shifting
his perspective abruptly, gives us a glimpse of the musician
whose song we have just heard:

> Thus sang the uncouth swain to th'oaks and rills,
> While the still morn went out with sandals gray;
> He touched the tender stops of various quills,
> With eager thought warbling his Doric lay.
> And now the sun had stretched out all the hills,
> And now was dropped into the western bay;
> At last he rose, and twitched his mantle blue:
> To-morrow to fresh woods, and pastures new.

It is true, as Mr. Wittreich has pointed out, that the rhymes in
these final eight lines mark a "concerted effort to return us to

the first movement, and then to the first lines of the poem."[11] But no rhyme scheme (even if we *could* hear a rhyme a hundred lines apart) can ever bring these eight lines into the perspective of the rest of the poem. For Milton is quite obviously focusing our attention on the imaginary nature of his vision, just as a novelist might tell us at the end of his story that the actions occurred in a dream. Of course such a distancing effect doesn't invalidate the vision, or make it trivial; it is not a mere dream. As Cleanth Brooks and J. E. Hardy have pointed out, the purpose of this focusing on the singer rather than on the song "is not to deny the vision of promise with which the elegy concludes, but only to place it definitely in that perspective which must be an essential part of its truth. . . . We are simply reminded that the vision is one of hope, not yet fulfilled, that the elegy has been composed and delivered in a real world in which suns rise and set, day follows day, the flood remains perilous to all those whom Lycidas has left behind, and the young shepherd has to bethink himself of the duties of the new day."[12]

To see the doctrine of immortality in this light, as part of an aesthetic experience in which the sense of reality, the "perilous flood," is also a meaningful part, is to read the poem figuratively rather than literally. And in doing so we may seem to lessen the seriousness of *Lycidas*. We are a long way from the attitude of those readers who, like Paul Elmer More, felt that "He who would read the poem worthily . . . must be equally sensitive to the delicacy of its art and the sublimity of its ideas."[13] But if the viewpoint presented here would make *Lycidas*, and all poetry, less *serious* in a moral or philosophical sense, it can also allow us to see its unique value. For any prose passage can express a sublime idea. What poetry can do is to give us ideas or myths that cannot be falsified because, unlike the ideas in philosophy or in religion, they do not have to be believed. For the ideas in literature form part of a pattern which is of value in itself. As Frank Kermode has recently reminded us, all men, in every age, "make considerable investments in coherent patterns, which, by provision of an end, make satisfying consonance with the origin and the middle. That is why the image of an end can never be permanently falsified."

But just as we need and accept this "satisfying consonance" in the image of Lycidas rising from his grave, to complete the cycle of his birth and his death, so we also, to quote Kermode again, "feel the need to show a marked respect for things as they are; so that there is a recurring need for adjustments in the interests of reality as well as of control."[14] The sense of "reality as well as of control" is particularly relevant to the final eight lines of *Lycidas*. Here we see made explicit what all readers have felt as they reread the poem: the unusually firm control of all the "tender stops" on the part of Milton.

The word *control* as well as the consonance of origins and ends, suggests music as well as literature, and few critics have been able to resist some reference to music in a discussion of *Lycidas*. Some of the connections are obvious, and perhaps superficial. When the poet impersonates a shepherd who "must sing for Lycidas," and who must "somewhat loudly sweep the string," we are, of course, only being reminded of the conventions of pastoral poetry. But this convention gains more significance when we see that Milton has made a deliberate effort to imitate musical forms, not only in rhyme and rhythm, but also in the development and the recapitulation of themes and images. The specific technical aspects of this relationship have been explored by a number of critics.[15] What concerns us here is that the constant reminders that this poem is a musical composition sharpens our awareness of the distance between the actual feelings and those created by the poem.

We would not deny that there are human emotions in music, or at least that most of us find such emotions in most of the music that we listen to. But we also would admit, even if we are not formalists, that in music, more than in any other art, the sadness, the gaiety, the sense of defeat and the sense of victory, of agitation and resignation, are felt only through sound. We *hear* the emotions. These emotions, whether they are in the music or only in those who listen to it, are embodied in sounds and rhythms. And we would also grant that the change from an *adagio* to an *allegro* or from a *forte* to a *pianissimo* is *not* a revelation of a change in the composer from sadness to joy, or from strength to weakness. Such simple correspondence may be discerned in some music, but surely the mark of good music is that it can inspire feelings that are so bound up with the specific pattern of sounds as to go beyond our everyday emotions. An *allegro* movement that follows an *andante* certainly is not a sign that the composer has transmuted grief into joy. Such terms would be too crude, certainly, to characterize the complex feelings that are inspired by great music. Nor do we make any sort of commitment, in the usual sense of that word, when our mood changes as we listen first to a funeral movement and then to a movement with more interesting rhythms and brighter sounds.

Music, quite obviously, is incapable of offering us a convincing reason for changing from one mood to another. We nevertheless recognize that some developments and resolutions are extremely satisfying, *appropriate*, or as we sometimes feel, *inevitable*. Granted that poetry is a different art, that it is the meaning not the sounds of words that is of paramount interest, the distancing effect is very much the same. When we are asked in *Lycidas* to "weep no more, for Lycidas your sorrow is not dead," we are not convinced by the truth or the sublimity of the Christian idea of immortality. If the grief in all of its forms has become embodied in the musical structure of the poem, as so many critics have shown us, then the tears that are wiped "for ever from his eyes," must also be part of that structure. It is not poetry that is brought into the higher syntheses of Christianity, but rather the Christian *consolatio* that is brought into the imaginative experience of the poem. And it is only within this world created by the poem, or more precisely by the "uncouth swain" who is fingering "the tender stops of various quills," that the tears are wiped away "for ever."

Within the actual world, the song or monody is over, and tomorrow, in the fresh woods and pastures, there may be other tears which may require other poetic forms to transmute them into "melodious tears." For poetry as well as music can, in Shelley's words, "marry grief and pleasure, eternity and change" and subdue "to union under its light yoke, all irreconcilable things." And we can guess, perhaps, that it is Milton's confidence in his poetic power rather than any confidence in the validity of any doctrine in the poem that allows him to go on "to fresh woods and pastures new." As for the modern reader, we can do more than guess. We can assert that the poem derives its power, not from the sublimity of its doctrine, but from Milton's ability to transmute that doctrine into an integral part of a musical structure.

NOTES

1. *Milton's Lycidas, The Tradition and the Poem*, ed. C. A. Patrides (New York, 1961), pp. 212–31. (This volume of essays will be referred to subsequently by the editor's name.)
2. Joseph Anthony Wittreich, Jr., "Milton's 'Destined Urn': The Art of *Lycidas*," PMLA 84 (January 1969), 67.
3. "'Eager Thought': Dialectic in *Lycidas*," PMLA 78 (1962), 27–32. Reprinted in *Milton, Modern Essays in Criticism*, ed. Arthur Barker (New York, 1965). Quotations are from this collection, pp. 114, 118.
4. Marjorie Nicolson, *John Milton, A Reader's Guide to His Poetry* (New York, 1963), p. 102.
5. *Images and Themes in Five Poems of Milton* (Cambridge, Mass., 1957), p. 87.
6. Ibid., p. 103.
7. "Approaches to 'Lycidas,'" *The Living Milton*, ed. Frank Kermode (London, 1960), p. 43.
8. Ibid., p. 53.
9. "The Pastoral Elegy and Milton's *Lycidas*," Patrides, op. cit., p. 55. (See note 1 above.) Originally printed in *PMLA* in 1910.
10. "Voice and Structure in *Lycidas*," *Texas Studies in Literature and Language* XII (Spring 1970), 21.
11. Wittreich, op. cit., p. 64.
12. Patrides, op. cit., p. 152. Originally printed in *The Poems of Mr. John Milton* (New York, 1951).
13. Patrides, op. cit., p. 94. Originally printed in the *American Review* in 1936.
14. *The Sense of An Ending* (New York, 1967), p. 17.
15. See particularly Gretchen Finney, *Musical Backgrounds for English Literature* (1580–1660) (New Brunswick, N.J., 1962); and Wittreich, note 2 above. For a less technical but masterful and sensitive account of the musical structure, see also that of Marjorie Nicolson in *A Readers Guide*, op. cit., pp. 105–111.

IV

Dogma and Poetry
in *Paradise Lost*

THAT WE GO to *Paradise Lost* for its poetry rather than for its theology is a truism and, at the same time, a distortion of the truth. It is a distortion of the truth for a number of reasons; but, most obviously, such a statement does not account for the fact that the poetry develops from a very elaborate set of dogmas. No matter how much we talk of patterns of imagery and of rhythm, of dramatic confrontations and vivid descriptions, no analysis of the poem can be at all adequate if it fails to take into account Milton's deliberate attempt to inculcate moral lessons. And it is this moral philosophy, or theology, this deliberate attempt of the poem's narrator to interpret our response to the action presented in the poem, that has caused many modern readers to be dissatisfied with the total effect of *Paradise Lost*. Perhaps the best known expression of this dissatisfaction was voiced some twenty years ago by A. J. A. Waldock when he argued that Milton's intention of justifying the ways of God is in conflict with the effect that the poem actually has on the reader.

> If we attend, not to the ghost epic, but to the epic that is there, on the pages, written, we shall feel at once, I think . . . a fundamental clash . . . between what the poem asserts, on the one hand, and what it compels us to feel, on the other. That is why we are uneasy, as at something wrong, deep down in the treatment and that is why *Paradise Lost* does not profoundly satisfy us in the manner of great tragedy; it cannot because of the embedded ambiguity at the heart of it.[1]

34

Without in any way attempting to summarize the main trends in twenty years of scholarship devoted to this epic, one can say that a good part of such scholarship has been directed to a refutation of this statement. By references to Milton's theology and to his tradition, by careful attention to the logic of God's arguments as compared to the specious reasonings of Satan (as well as by jeremiads against the inability of modern readers to see the real virtue of obedience), scholars and critics have tried to show that there is indeed a harmony, and not a disjunction, between what Milton intended us to feel and what the action of the poem causes us to feel. But like Waldock, these scholars assume that the readers must be willing to share, if only imaginatively, Milton's basic assumptions about morality.

There is something to be said for much of the work that has been done in this tradition. And my own reading of the poem will reveal my debt to these critics. I also share with these critics the feeling that, contrary to Waldock's statement, *Paradise Lost* has nothing wrong "deep down" and that it does in fact (or at least it can) "profoundly satisfy" a modern reader of poetry. What I question, however, is the assumption of traditional scholarship that we can (by scholarly probing of Milton's theological tradition), or that we should (by a justification of traditional Christian morality), feel just what the narrator of the poem tells us to feel. Whether the narrator is simply John Milton, or the "blind bard," there is no reason to assume that he "controls the mood and meaning of every scene in the poem," as Anne Ferry has maintained.[2] On the contrary, the assertions of the narrator are part of the dramatic scene; we should interpret his moralizing in the light of what actually happens, and not the other way around. We will then see that the contrast between what we ought to feel according to the explicit statements of the narrator and what Adam and Eve actually do feel, far from destroying the poem, gives it a dramatic tension that transforms the dogma into poetry. With such a reading *Paradise Lost* can satisfy us, not as a moral commentary, but, as Waldock demands, "satisfy us in the manner of great tragedy."

But this transformation of the dogma into poetry cannot occur until we give up our tendency to judge the doctrines on the basis of their philosophical or moral values and think of them simply as material out of which the drama is formed. Such an attitude does not in any way detract from the meaning or the importance of these dogmas. A contextualist aesthetics does not, or at least should not, ignore the meaning of the work in order to concentrate on its form. It is only that we want to see the meaning of a passage or of a scene not in terms of its relation to our world or to Milton's world, but in relation to the total action within the poem. And within the poem a doctrine or an action is right or wrong because of what has gone before and because of what is to come. To the extent that we are within the poem we are concerned with *why* certain things are said and done, and not with their moral or logical validity. The dogma in *Paradise Lost* is important, as it would be in any work, not as a guide to conduct but for its use in the dramatic action that unfolds before us. And once we comprehend the dramatic action, we will see that the meaning of the poem is something quite different from the meanings that go into the poem. We will then be able, as we mentioned earlier, "to see what was *not* in existence before the poem was completed."

Such a view of *Paradise Lost* is implicit in a number of interpretations, and references will be made to them. The study of Milton's language, particularly, has helped us to focus our attention on what Milton has created rather than on the concepts that Milton has taken from the literary and religious traditions. But both critics and readers are still troubled by the gap between the dogmatic assertions of the narrator and the actions of the leading characters which seem to contradict these assertions. It is hard to deny, despite the arguments of William Empson, that Milton is constantly striving to make his readers see the justice of God's ways, no matter how arbitrary they may seem. At the same time, despite the efforts of orthodox critics (particularly Miltonists on this side of the Atlantic), it is impossible to overlook Milton's equally strong need to question the actions of God, to face clearly the obvious contradictions between God's ways and our own human standards of justice and rationality. What I hope to do here is to show that this conflict is not a weakness in *Paradise Lost* but the source of its strength. For it is not Milton's doctrine but his strong doubts about the doctrine that provide the emotional center of the poem. Only by responding to Milton's doubts as well as to his certainties, and by accepting both the rebellion and the submission *without* trying to reconcile them, can we do justice to the imaginative experience of the poem.

It may seem strange to assert that God's ways are meant to appear incomprehensible in a Christian epic. But the word Christianity has a number of meanings, not all of which are related to the doctrines. The many doctrines that have appeared in the Christian tradition are of course important, and Milton puts into his poem most of the elements of the Protestant dogma. But Christianity can also refer to the literary and historical record that has come down to us in the legends of the Old and New Testaments. In this sense Christianity is not so much a doctrine which tells us what we must do to be saved, but a collection of stories and poems, dreams and historical fragments that relate man's deepest personal experiences to the entire universe. There is, consequently, not only a Christian doctrine about which we can agree or disagree, but a Christian myth that, like all myths, can link human desires and fears with the natural world, and our immediate life with the infinite past and infinite future. As Wayne Shumaker has said: "No matter how richly the narrative events are overlaid with reason, it is by the events themselves that the structure of the known universe has been determined."[3]

It is true that Milton is not merely presenting the Christian myth, but the theology which interprets this myth. As Isabel MacCaffrey has pointed out: "The myth in the poem has been assimilated into a larger design, which cannot be called mythical in any sense acceptable to modern theory; it becomes part of a moral pattern that is actually anti-mythical. . . . It is to be turned into religion, made to accommodate a theology."[4] However, we need not assume that the assimilation is a one-way process. The Christian myth that we find here is too powerful to be completely absorbed in the theology; in fact, as we will try to show here, the theology is *inadequate* to accommodate the myth. For the theology in *Paradise Lost* cannot account for the arbitrary actions of God, or for the feeling that the Satanic forces in the poem (whether in Satan himself or in Adam and

Eve) are as attractive to the reader as the forces of Heaven. Far from being "assimilated into a larger design," the mythical elements of *Paradise Lost* are in constant opposition to the Christian theology. This opposition, or dualism, has been noticed by readers for over two centuries, and has been accounted for in innumerable ways. What I hope to do here is to show how this dualism can be seen not so much as a problem but as a central fact in the imaginative experience of the poem. The most obvious focus for this problem is Milton's portrait of Satan.

The indomitable will, the courage never to submit or yield, the sheer energy that runs through the lines of Books I and II have been admired by so many readers and analyzed by so many critics that no more need be said here about the powerful effect of Satan. But if one is bound by the Christian doctrine, which is expressed most obviously by the narrator of the poem, the heroic energy of Satan does indeed become a problem. Since we must, according to the dogma, condemn and despise Satan, many critics have stretched their ingenuity to prove that Satan's courage, daring, and intelligence are only apparent, and that our admiration for him should give way to feelings of scorn and contempt. One critic has gone so far as to question the reality of Satan's actions: "The typical demonic 'act' is not a real act either, but is a much more concentrated parody of divine action." It is only Christ who can act, "as the agent or acting principle of the Father, he is ultimately the only actor in the poem."[5] Of course, by "ultimately" or "real," the critic means in accordance with some doctrinal truth. If theological truth is the reality of the poem and the actions are merely clothing, the critics are quite right in looking *through,* not at the actions and speeches of Satan and his followers. But for a literary interpretation, we need no such distinction between the outward appearance and inner reality. Everything in a poem is real. The actions of Satan do not then have to be explained away, but accepted as being just as much a part of Milton's universe as the actions of God. In such an interpretation, since we are concerned with the myth rather than the theology of Christianity, we can see Hell and Heaven, evil and good, not only as polar opposites but as interdependent forces.

The differences between God and His great adversary have been pointed out by many critics. Satan is defeated while God is triumphant; Satan is stirred up by envy and revenge, filled with mortal hate, while God is the source of love and mercy. Satan is surrounded by darkness, while God is, of course, the embodiment of light. But the similarities between the two opposing forces are just as strong: Satan may be defeated in separate battles, but he wages an unrelenting war against God which eventually succeeds in bringing Sin and Death into Eden, God's noblest creation. Even the contrast between revenge and mercy can also be seen as a similarity. From the viewpoint of Adam and Eve, God's actions towards them after they have eaten the apple is a form of revenge; and the mercy of God occurs only after He punishes them. But the Fall will be discussed in the next chapter. Here we are concerned with the interdependence of Good and Evil before the eating of the apple. And our first example is the portrait of Satan.

Not only the action but the language helps to create a sense of continuity between the two polar opposites. The "darkness visible," surrounding Satan, flames with an intensity that anticipates the brightness of God, which is also a kind of darkness, since it would blind the ordinary eye and can only "Shine inward." As Jackson Cope has pointed out with great thoroughness, the basic images of the poem, light and darkness, sight and blindness, rising and falling, are used by Milton not only as antithetical elements but as part of a cyclical rhythm that runs through the poem. Light is the opposite of darkness, but "light carries the potential of darkness, as sight carries the potential of blindness." This paradox is appropriate also to the interdependence of God and Satan. "God is victor, but He is victor upon terms of Satan's instrumentality. Man's resurrection will coincide with Satan's final fall, but only after Satan's rising has occasioned man's Fall."[6]

This cyclical rhythm created by light and darkness is given a further interpretation by Philip Brockbank who traces the conflict between Satan and God to its source in nature itself. Quoting the lines from Isaiah (XIV:12–13), "How art thou fallen from Heaven, O Lucifer, son of the morning! how art thou cut down to the ground, which didst weaken the nations! For thou hast said in thine heart. I will ascend into heaven, I will exalt my throne above the stars of God . . . ," Mr. Brockbank comments as follows: "It is a central mystery of the phenomenal

world and of our metaphorical thinking that light and darkness
seem to be both complementary and contending essences. . . ."[7]

Writing from a different viewpoint, Roy Daniells comes to a
similar conclusion about Satan's relationship to God. Interested
particularly in the sense of power that dominates the poem
(and placing it in the baroque tradition), Professor Daniells
emphasizes the similarity between God and Satan in their "as-
sertion of the individual self and the achievement of superiority
over other selves. . . . Satan then demonstrates to the fullest
degree the trilogy of unity, power and will, by his own positive
exercise of these or his struggle to attain them or, conversely,
because at all points his negation reveals the positive of God:
true unity, beneficent power, and eternal will."[8] That God's
power is "beneficent" in contrast to Satan's does not negate the
fact that both forces are equally intent on power and will. We
are told, of course, by the narrator that God and Satan are
completely opposed; but what we see is the amazing similarity
and interdependence.

This interdependence of the opposing forces occurs not only
in the struggle between Satan and God, but also within Satan
himself. In the opening soliloquy of Book IV, Satan reveals his
recognition of God's beneficence and takes upon himself all the
blame for the revolt. Yet Satan asserts his pride even when he
laments that

> pride and worse ambition threw me down
> Warring in heav'n against heav'n's matchless King.
> Ah wherefore? He deserved no such return
> From me, whom he created what I was
> In that bright eminence, and with his good
> Upbraided none; nor was his service hard.
> What could be less than to afford him praise,
> The easiest recompense, and pay him thanks
> How due! . . . (40–48)

We can feel only pity for a rebel angel who is forced or tricked
into revolt by an inscrutable God. But what can we feel for an
angel who openly admits that his rebellion is an act of his own
free will, who absolves his enemy of all blame, and who shows
such haughty disdain of any kind of subjection?

Yet all his good proved ill in me,
And wrought but malice; lifted up so high
I sdained subjection, and thought one step higher
Would set me highest, and in a moment quit
The debt immense of endless gratitude,
So burthensome still paying, still to owe. . . . (48–53)

Surely, however we describe our response to this speech, we should allow for the fact that the heroic and the destructive aspects are both present in Satan. On the verge of committing his great sin against man and God, Satan is taking all the guilt upon himself, and is willing to endure the greatest suffering as a necessary penalty for his pride. Even Douglas Bush, whose notes continually warn us not to be taken in by the attractive qualities of the fiend, seems to allow some sense of greatness to Satan at this moment, noting that "his pangs of conscience in relation to God give him tragic potentialities that set him apart from his fellows; these however, are not allowed to develop."[9]

From a theological perspective the greatness is indeed a problem; and Douglas Bush, like many Miltonists who see the poem as an exemplification of the doctrine, must keep Satan from becoming a tragic figure. But from the literary perspective the tragic stature of Satan is not a problem but is consistent with the pattern of the entire poem. Just as the light served to bring forth darkness which in turn brings forth a greater light (as we have seen earlier in the quotation from Jackson Cope) so the greatness of Satan's character makes his debt, at this point, more burdensome. His desire to exercise all of the potentialities of his being is remarkably similar to God's desire to fill the void with His divine being. Within such a perspective we can enjoy rather than be embarrassed by the power and sensitivity of Satan. We can accept rather than try to explain away the impression of almost all readers, expressed so well by Helen Gardner: "The doomed, obstinate figure of Satan, persisting with such energy and fortitude and disdain of pain . . . in his destructive and self-destructive course, has the grandness of the tragic, the exceptional, the thing that is greater than we are."[10]

All of these qualities, the heroic and the embittered, the sense of defeat and the sense of glory, can be seen in these famous lines:

So farewell hope, and with hope farewell fear,
Farewell remorse! All good to me is lost;
Evil be thou my good; by thee at least
Divided empire with heav'n's King I hold
By thee, and more than half perhaps will reign;
As man ere long, and this new world shall know. (108–13)

So great is the interdependence of good and evil here that evil
literally becomes Satan's "good." To continue the paradox, Satan
will divide the rule of the universe with "heav'n's King," by
losing all that is good and embracing evil. In this situation we
should not be surprised to find that the farewell to hope is made
with as much strength and eagerness as is the farewell to
fear. But for the full development of the paradox in which evil
becomes good, we must follow Satan into Eden. The transition
is of course a logical one in many ways. This "happy rural seat"
created by God out of His goodness was of course also created to
take the place of the rebellious angels. Satan then belongs in
Eden in this ironic sense also. We should also remember
(from Book III) that God has already foreseen that Adam and
Eve will succumb to Satan and that their innocence shall give
way to a knowledge of good and evil. From its very inception,
therefore, this garden is both an untroubled Paradise with perfect creatures as its inhabitants and, at the same time, a battleground between its two creators, God and Satan.

But although Eden is now a battleground (as are Hell and
Heaven) between Satan and God, the battle itself takes a very
different form. From an external, military warfare in which
armed legions fought in "dubious battle," we come now to an
inward struggle in which the forces of good and evil fight within
the soul of man. This inward struggle completely changes the
role of Satan. Only in brief moments does Satan revert to his
early heroic self; from now on his significant actions are in the
guise of a toad or serpent. But this decline in the stature of
Satan does not imply, as some commentators believe, a decline
in the Satanic forces. The desire to revolt against the fixed,
hierarchical order of God, the desire to express all of the potentialities of the universe—the evil and the destructive as well as
the good—is by no means diminished by Satan's transition from
a general to a toad. Only now these Satanic forces are within

Adam and Eve, particularly Eve. And since our first parents are created by God, in His image (even if Eve is so indirectly), Adam and Eve also represent the obedience, humility, and spirituality that are the opposite of the Satanic forces. Thus by becoming embodied in the very soul of Adam and Eve, as well as in the relationship between them, the polar opposites which have hitherto been represented by Heaven and Hell are now brought together.

The interdependence of good and evil that we have seen in the complementarity between God and Satan is now seen in the complementary relationship between Adam and Eve. And, as the characters develop, we shall see that good and evil, the opposing forces of pride and humility, reason and passion, struggle for mastery within them as well. The "dubious battle on the plains of heav'n" will continue to shake the throne of the Almighty, but the battle will now take place within the minds and hearts of Adam and Eve. If we thus recognize Eden as another stage in the great conflict that rages throughout the poem, in Heaven, in Hell, and on earth, we shall not be troubled by the fact that sinful impulses and conflict are clearly present even in the state of innocence.

The first description of Adam as being subservient to God only, while Eve is created "for God in him," whose "eye sublime declared/Absolute rule," makes clear immediately that the question of obedience that brought about the war in heaven is still with us here. What is even more interesting in terms of the structure of the poem is that as soon as we see the noble pair in "youthful dalliance," we are also presented with Satan's introductory words: "O hell! what do mine eyes with grief behold!" (358) There is an obvious irony in that Satan can never experience love, only hate. But the deeper irony is that this perfect love between Adam and Eve, with their "endearing smiles," is a premonition of their fall. Adam's deepest and noblest feeling becomes, as we shall soon see, the cause of his disobedience to God. The love that God grants to Adam as His greatest gift, the love that allows Adam and Eve to be "Imparadised in one another's arms," brings about *their* Hell as well as the "Hell" which Satan gives expression to at the present moment.

This duality in their love is linked to the duality in their freedom. Since there is no genuine love for God if it is forced or constrained in any way, God left free the will. What God had said about the angels in Book III applies equally to man:

> Freely they stood who stood, and fell who fell
> Not free, what proof could they have giv'n sincere
> Of true allegiance, constant faith or love. . . . (102–104)

But it is this very freedom that allows man to disobey God. Just as the heroic quality in Satan—his unconquerable will—is also the quality that dooms him to ultimate perdition, so the highest qualities that Milton can imagine in the perfect man and woman are the very qualities that destroy this perfection. Some critics would argue that it is not the love and the freedom that destroy the garden but the perversion of these qualities. It is only when free will is turned into ambition and love into lust, they maintain, that paradise is lost. But such an interpretation, convincing enough in a verbal sense, does not, I hope to show here, take into account the continuity between love and lust, freedom and rebellion, which pervades the actions of our first parents.

When Eve recounts her first experience, or at least the first that she remembers, her rebellious spirit can be seen in her preference for her own image over Adam's. Of course when she is told that she is meant for Adam, she gladly submits to him:

> I yielded, and from that time see
> How beauty is excelled by manly grace
> And wisdom, which alone is truly fair. (489–91)

But the submission does not remove the impulse towards independence; and we are reminded that the seeds of conflict are inherent in Paradise. The fact that Eve and even Adam indicate sinful tendencies in their unfallen condition, has been, as was mentioned above, an important problem to those critics who want to see in the poem a clear-cut division between good and evil. It is a problem for the majority of critics for the same reason that it is a problem for a theologian, or for anyone who attempts to explain logically how perfectly innocent man can be seduced into sin. But if we look at the poem as a myth, as a story that attempts to give narrative form to our deepest impulses, there is no problem. For the story of Eden as presented here does justice to both our dream of a perfect state and our sense that this state, if it existed at all, was transitory and that it could realize its potentialities only in experience. The innocence as presented here is part of the cyclical rhythm that permeates the entire poem: just as light gives way to darkness, the upward movement to a downward movement, so innocence realizes its full potentiality by moving towards experience.

This duality in Eden has been seen by a number of critics, particularly those who have examined the language of the poem. As Arnold Stein has said: "Paradise is a compressed myth of natural sympathy and order, between light and darkness, between the waters below and the waters above; growing things are blessedly in the center, thirsting downwards for darkness and earth and water, thirsting upward for light and sky and water."[11] Even Mrs. MacCaffrey, who emphasizes the sharp demarcation between the fallen and unfallen worlds, nevertheless sees an ambivalence in the idea of a perfect Eden: "within the depths of Paradise, there is a corruption, making creation in a sense 'imperfect.' " And this imperfection is given added force by the sense of abundance in Eden. In commenting upon the line "Wild above rule or art; enormous bliss," Mrs. MacCaffrey finds another example of the sense of corruption that is potentially present even in Paradise: "Milton was always conscious of the meanings of his Latin words, and intended them to be operative in the poem. In *enormous,* he has reiterated the idea that paradisal nature was 'above' rule."[12]

It is inevitable that modern readers will see a psychological analogue in the myth of Eden, as well as in the great emphasis which Milton places on the contrast between light and darkness, and the upward and downward movements. And if we follow such a lead, and relate darkness and the downward movement to the unconscious in man, it becomes easier to understand why darkness and downward motion are not necessarily evil. For mysterious and "dark" as it may be, what lies below our conscious level is as necessary for the completeness of our lives as our conscious desires. Again Mrs. MacCaffrey's description of this aspect of the poem is most perceptive: "Struggle, tempta-

tion, resistance were everywhere, imbedded in the very structure of macrocosm and microcosm. The constant presence of
some sort of 'abyss' in *Paradise Lost* is a reminder that the
possibility of the fall is never far away. The inclusion of
darkness in the very midst of light is, too, appropriate to the
tensions of a mythic world where all the events of history are
held in embryo."[13]

The possibilities for destruction, for temptation and resistance to God, are inherent not only in Eden itself but in the
very qualities that are noblest in man. Even the love between
Adam and Eve reaches its full potentialities only when it becomes destructive, as we shall see in Book IX. But Satan sees it
already as he watches Adam and Eve embrace:

> He [Adam] in delight
> Both of her beauty and her submissive charms
> Smiled with superior love, as Jupiter
> On Juno smiles, when he impregns the clouds
> That shed May flowers; and pressed her matron lip
> With kisses pure. (497–502)

To Satan this sight is hateful and tormenting, and he watches
with envy "these two/Imparadised in one another's arms."
And in Book IX, of course, it will become clear just how
this embrace can remove the very paradise that is now being
created within the hearts and minds of Adam and Eve. But as
we see through the eyes of Satan, we become aware that the
destruction of this innocent love is inherent in the innocence
itself. For Satan quickly sees that the potentiality of knowledge
(and also, as we shall see, of carnal knowledge) must destroy
innocence. How can we have perfect happiness rest on ignorance? If man is given reason, Satan argues in a tone reminiscent
of the *Areopagitica*, why should full possibilities of this
reason not be developed?

> Knowledge forbidden?
> Suspicious, reasonless. Why should their Lord
> Envy them that? Can it be sin to know
> Can it be death? And do they only stand
> By ignorance, is that their happy state,
> The proof of their obedience and their faith? (515–20)

Milton's own attitude towards knowledge throughout *Paradise Lost* (as well as throughout his life) has been discussed at great length by many scholars. A great deal of ingenuity has been expended in trying to reconcile Milton's obvious regard for learning and his own unbounded intellectual curiosity with his acceptance of the Biblical concept of a forbidden knowledge. But the conflict and reconciliation within Milton does not affect our interpretation of this scene. For however the conflict may have been reconciled in Milton's mind or in his actions, it is clear that there is no conciliation between freedom and forbidden knowledge here in Eden. Nor should we look for one. For it is this conflict that gives the scene its dramatic intensity and its intellectual excitement. Whether Satan is right in his argument, or wrong, is of interest to us only outside of the poem. Within the imaginative experience we are not concerned with the validity of his argument but with the simple and unchanging fact that man must remain ignorant in order to reach his greatest happiness. At the time, again within the context of the poem (not only in our own secular minds), we are made to feel that man's reason is a sign of his godlike nature, as well as being a sheer delight in itself. Adam, we must remember, speaks about astronomy with almost as much pleasure as he speaks about his love for Eve. Our sympathy with Satan's argument, therefore, is not caused by a fault in us, or in the poet. We are supposed to feel the contradiction implicit in the myth, a contradiction whose sharpness is expressed by the narrator himself when he states that the best knowledge for the innocent pair is to "know to know no more." (775) What is significant about Satan's comment, therefore, is not the validity or the speciousness of his reasoning, but the presentation of a truth that underlies the paradox of the state of innocence. That God gives man reason as His highest gift and then forbids man to exercise it to its limit is indeed a "fair foundation laid whereon to build/Their ruin!" (521)

The pain and the joy of this state of innocence come together in an even more complex relationship in the next scene, in which Adam and Eve discuss the nature of the universe and exemplify the nature of human love. The alternation of day and night as described by Adam to his consort makes intellectual

activity seem to be an uninhibited delight. But Eve reminds
him that, at least for women, there is a limit to knowledge:
"God is thy law, thou mine; to know no more/Is woman's hap-
piest knowledge and her praise" (637–38). She then goes on to
her famous lines "With thee conversing I forget all time . . .,"
and we learn that although she is willing to accept a limitation
on intellectual knowledge, she is not aware of any limitation on
their love for each other. As they go "hand in hand . . . On to the
blissful bower" (689–90), there seems to be no reason for God
to put any limitation on the knowledge to be gained through
sexual or through intellectual activity. But of course God does
put strict limits on these impulses. And we are given a hint of
this danger even as we witness them in their nuptial bower:

> Here in close recess
> With flowers, garlands, and sweet-smelling herbs
> Espousèd Eve decked first her nuptial bed,
> And heav'nly quires the hymenean sung,
> What day the genial angel to our sire
> Brought her in naked beauty more adorned,
> More lovely than Pandora, whom the gods
> Endowed with all their gifts, and O too like
> In sad event, when to the unwiser son
> Of Japhet brought by Hermes, she ensnared
> Mankind with her fair looks, to be avenged
> On him who had stole Jove's authentic fire. (708–719)

It is precisely at the best moments, at the very height of their
bliss, that the image of Pandora steals in to remind us that the
sense of loss comes about when we possess everything, that
paradise is being lost when it is held most closely. Yet, we are
constantly told, this state is decreed by an all-powerful and all-
merciful God whose actions can be justified to men. Of course
we are troubled by such a situation. But so is Milton. And in
Book VIII, we are presented with a dramatic representation of
those contradictions that have been increasingly evident as the
poem develops.

When Adam opens the discussion of astronomy by asking
Raphael just why the earth should be the center of the solar
system, Eve walks away. But we are quickly told that she is no

less capable than Adam of enjoying intellectual discourse; but she prefers to hear the discourse from her husband. That knowledge is also an angelic delight is seen in the eloquence with which Raphael delineates both the geocentric and the heliocentric pictures of the solar system. Marjorie Nicolson has shown us how great was Milton's interest in the new astronomy, and how profoundly the discoveries of Galileo and others affected the sense of space that permeates the entire poem.[14] Even the technical details of astronomy stimulate his imagination: the swift motion of the various spheres in the Ptolemaic system as well as the possibility (in the Copernican system) that the other stars dance around the sun "By his attractive virtue and their own/Incited" (124–25), are almost suggested by the vigorous movement of the verse. Yet at the end of this discourse, Raphael tells Adam that his knowledge is both trivial and sinful! "Solicit not thy thoughts with matters hid:/Leave them to God above, him serve and fear" (167–68). What is even more surprising is that even before he begins his long and vivid astronomical explanation, Raphael warns Adam that "From man or angel the great Architect/Did wisely conceal and not divulge" the secrets of heavenly motion (72–73).

Adam is in no way disturbed by these contradictory attitudes. In fact, he reveals the same contradiction. First he agrees with Raphael that we should avoid "perplexing thoughts" and be happy "not to know at large of things remote/From use." At the same time, however, Adam can hardly wait to tell the story of his own creation. It is true that man's creation is described as being of "A lower flight" and as dealing not with the obscure but with "things at hand/Useful" (200). But the explanation is not convincing. The creation of Adam and Eve is as remote from Raphael as the heavenly bodies are from Adam; and astronomy, at least in some of its aspects, is more useful to man than man's early history is to an angel.

There is no getting around the fact that we are presented with two very different attitudes towards knowledge. There is a logical difficulty for any reader who tries to reconcile the injunctions against knowledge with the manifest delight in intellectual activity that is presented here. For those critics who try to

decide which attitude towards knowledge the poet really favors,
or which attitude the reader should adopt, the difficulty is even
greater. To debate the merits of knowledge *per se* is to leave the
context of the poem and get into a moral debate. But the
literary critic is not the judge of the respective merits of the two
attitudes towards knowledge. For a literary appreciation of
the poem we have no need to take sides; we need only accept
the fact that Milton presents us with a dilemma that is to have
grave consequences for the future action of the poem. The
delight in intellectual exploration of even the most abstruse
matters, as well as a distrust of what is subtle and remote, are
both deeply rooted in man. God has given man great confidence
in the use of his reason and an equally great fear of the consequences of unbounded reason. God may very well know just
what He is doing and why, as we are told often enough throughout the book. But God's explanation does not prevent Adam,
nor should it prevent the reader, from recognizing the contradiction. For Adam is in a state of innocence, a state in which
knowledge and the desire for knowledge can only be linked to
goodness. Only after he has fallen can Adam really understand
what Raphael means when he talks about a knowledge that is
sinful. It is not that Adam is wrong and Raphael is right, or vice
versa; what we see is that they are speaking from different view-
points. (Not that Raphael is a fallen angel, but he speaks with
the knowledge of the Fall). Adam can only learn to "know no
more" when he has known too much.

This paradox continues when we move on to the second part
of the book where Adam asks Raphael for knowledge not about
the stars but about the proper relationship between husband
and wife. Before doing so, Adam tries to satisfy the angel's
curiosity about the origins of man. The most significant point in
this story occurs when Adam asks God for a mate: "In soli-
tude/What happiness? Who can enjoy alone" (364–65). God
pretends to dispute this argument for a moment, but soon
admits that Adam is right, and announces that He, God, knew it
all along: "I ere thou spak' It/Knew it not good for man to
be alone" (444–45). And we then get Adam's own account of
the creation of Eve:

The rib he formed and fashioned with his hands;
Under his forming hands a creature grew,
Man-like, but different sex, so lovely fair
That what seemed fair in all the world seemed now
Mean...."   (469-73)

Like the God who created him, Adam is perfect and yet needs
something outside of himself to fulfill his potentialities. Eve
is both outside of Adam and yet still part of him: "Man-like,
but different sex." She too is created by God—"under his forming hands." God again is responsible for what gives Adam his
greatest and noblest delight, and also for what will prove the
cause of his downfall. Eve's difference from Adam, to continue
the paradox, is the reason for his losing Paradise. But it is also
this very difference which, although it leaves her "the inferior in
the mind/And inward faculties," also accounts for her at-
traction: "So lovely fair/That what seemed fair in all the world
seemed now" inferior. That Eve is taken from Adam's rib is not
only a legend that Milton used, but is a perfect metaphor for
the closeness between them. This dependence on Eve is given its
strongest expression in the lines which conclude Adam's
account of her appearance in his dream:

She disappeared, and left me dark; I waked
To find her, or forever to deplore
Her loss, and other pleasures all abjure.... (478-80)

With these lines echoing in our mind, perhaps the most
memorable lines in the entire Book, we should not be surprised
that Adam soon finds that "All higher knowledge in her
presense falls/Degraded" (551-52), particularly when this
higher knowledge decrees that Eve is "th' inferior in the mind/
And inward faculties" (541-42). For there is no sharp separation between the mind and the body here. God has not only
made Eve "so lovely fair," but He has made sexuality an expression of the highest feelings that Adam is capable of. The physical union of Adam and Eve, as we saw in Book IV, is approved
of by the heavens themselves:

> all heav'n
> And happy constellations on that hour
> Shed their selectest influence; the earth
> Gave sign of gratulation, and each hill;
> Joyous the birds; fresh gales and gentle airs
> Whispered it to the woods, and from their wings
> Flung rose, flung odors from the spicy shrub,
> Disporting, till the amorous bird of night
> Sung spousal, and bid haste the ev'ning star
> On his hill top, to light the bridal lamp. (511–20)

Yet while Milton is doing everything in his poetic power to make us feel the beauty and innocence of this physical union, he is also reminding us that this love is dangerous. The feeling that allows Adam to experience his greatest ecstasy is also threatening to disturb the hierarchy of man and woman, reason and emotion:

> yet when I approach
> Her loveliness, so absolute she seems
> And in herself complete, so well to know
> Her own, that what she wills to do or say
> Seems wisest, virtuousest, discreetest, best;
> All higher knowledge in her presence falls
> Degraded. . . . (546–52)

That Adam should (or should not) have allowed his love for Eve to go as far as it did is irrelevant. Our saying that Adam is right or wrong, or whatever, reveals only our own sentiments. The literary significance lies in the undisputed fact that God has allowed this contradiction in Adam's make-up, that God took from Adam's side "More than enough" or else gave Eve too much beauty (535–39). (Of course Adam is tactful and says "Nature" not God "failed in me." But this tact does not fool Raphael, who tries to justify Nature as if it were God.) The nature of love, Raphael admits, does allow for the subjection of the lover. But this subjection is not necessary; for one can love in such a way as to maintain the superiority of reason over passion. And the angel goes on to make a careful and traditional distinction between the love that is dominated by sexuality and the love which "refines/The thoughts . . . hath his seat/In reason" (589–92) and is the first step on the ladder to heavenly love.

Raphael's argument is logical and eloquent. But again we are not responding correctly if we deliberate about its validity. A literary critic is not a judge of the relationship between passion and love, anymore than any other reader. The critic can only relate this conflict to the entire poem. In doing so, we can see how the greatest delight which is given to man can be in opposition to an even higher gift of the gods: "All higher knowledge in her presence falls/Degraded." And believing in a just and rational God, Adam cannot accept this contradiction. Why should man's spiritual ascent to "Heavenly Love" be in opposition to his physical love? Why should man's physical love be compared to that of the beasts? To Raphael's sharp distinction between the sexual and the spiritual, Adam counters with the concept of continuity between them. The "genial bed" in itself has a mysterious reverence and is in no way opposed to

> those graceful acts,
> Those thousand decencies that daily flow
> From all her words and actions, mixed with love
> And sweet compliance, which declare unfeigned
> Union of mind, or in both one soul. . . . (600–604)

We shall soon see that Eve's "sweet compliance" is contrary to her desire for equality and freedom, and how impossible it is for two individuals exercising their free will to maintain that "Union of mind" and body. But at this point Adam is aware of no such incompatibility. He is aware of a conflict between two of his strongest impulses; but since he is not aware of sin, he still believes that they can be reconciled. He is therefore unconvinced by Raphael's argument and feels free to "approve the best, and follow what I approve." So firm is his confidence in the continuity between the physical and the spiritual that he concludes his answer to Raphael by asking him whether sexuality exists among the angels. Raphael's reply assures him that it does; and such an answer would tend to support Adam's confidence in the goodness of sexuality. Of course Raphael also warns him again of the danger of passion: "take heed lest passion

sway/Thy judgment" (635–36). But passion, as Raphael defines
it, belongs to sinful man, and Adam cannot, at this point, really
understand him.

Taken out of the context of the poem, Raphael's argument
can be defended logically, morally, and even psychologically.
But to prove that one ought to act a certain way is not what a
poem does. And *Paradise Lost* is primarily a poem—a tragic
drama—and not a sermon. Adam's desire to reconcile the conflicting forces of reason and passion is at the same time admirable
and impossible. He is trying to hold on to Paradise while we are
being told here, and everywhere throughout the poem, that
Paradise is disappearing from the moment of its inception.
Paradise is constantly moving towards the world as we know it.
Milton is not taking sides between Raphael and Adam. The
poet expects us to share Adam's desire to keep the harmonious
union of man and woman, reason and passion, so that there may
be "one soul . . . in wedded pair." At the same time, and
this is the source of the dramatic tension, we are told by Raphael of the impossibility of such a harmony: "In loving thou dost
well, in passion not,/Wherein true love consists not. . . . " For
Adam, however, his passion for Eve, their delight in sexuality,
the "mysterious reverence" of "the genial bed" is an integral
part of that "Union of mind" which makes up the complete
"Harmony . . . in wedded pair." (604-5) Adam's tragedy does
not lie in his making the wrong choice, but in trying to hold
together impulses which are equally powerful and, as we shall
see in the next chapter, inherently incompatible.

NOTES

1. *Paradise Lost and Its Critics* (Cambridge, 1947), p. 145.
2. *Milton's Epic Voice* (Cambridge, Mass., 1963), p. 15.
3. *Unpremeditated Verse* (Princeton, 1967), p. 6.
4. Isabel MacCaffrey, *Paradise Lost as "Myth,"* (Cambridge, Mass., 1959),
p. 208.
5. Northrop Frye, *The Return of Eden* (Toronto, 1965), pp. 22–24.
6. *The Metaphoric Structure of Paradise Lost* (Baltimore, 1962), pp.
128, 123.
7. " 'Within the Visible Diurnal Sphere': The Moving World of *Paradise
Lost,*" in *Approaches to Paradise Lost,* ed. C. A. Patrides (London, 1968),
p. 207.

8. *Milton, Mannerism and Baroque* (Toronto, 1963), pp. 81, 110.
9. Douglas Bush, *The Complete Poetical Works of John Milton* (Boston, 1965), p. 275.
10. *A Reading of Paradise Lost* (Toronto, 1965), p. 76.
11. *Answerable Style* (Minneapolis, 1953), p. 65.
12. MacCaffrey, op. cit., pp. 153–54.
13. Ibid. p. 166.
14. "Milton and the Telescope," *ELH* (1953), 1–32. Reprinted in *Science and Imagination* (Ithaca, N.Y., 1956).

V

Dogma and Poetry in *Paradise Lost* Books IX and X

IN THE PRECEDING chapter I have described the main conflict in the poem as arising from the fact that the universe which God has created and which He governs cannot be reconciled with human standards of reason and justice. I have also tried to show that this contradiction between God's ways and our human values is not a weakness in the poem but the source of its dramatic power. For by giving full and unqualified expression to his feeling that God's actions are irrational and cruel and to his equally strong feeling that God is just and merciful, Milton is satisfying impulses that are deeply rooted in all men. Our evidence for this universal tendency to hold on to these contradictory feelings is based on the importance of myth, and of mythic thought. And by references to Milton's language, we have tried to show that the Christian myth in *Paradise Lost*, like myths in general, embodies contradictory feelings towards God and Satan and towards good and evil. By making use of the Christian myth, rather than Christian theology, Milton was able to show us the grandeur and heroic energy of Satan while at the same time (even in the same line) reminding us that Satan is an enemy to all that we hold good.

It is not that Satan is good and that God is evil; there is no doubt as to which is good. The ambivalence in the poem occurs because good itself—as exemplified in God, Heaven, light, upward movements, innocence—is so closely related to evil that we feel their opposition. God requires Satan for the completion of His universe, just as light requires darkness, innocence requires experience and, as we shall now see in Book IX, obedience requires disobedience. Thus, when we come to the climax of the

56

poem, we should not be surprised to find, as many critics have already found, that the fall of Adam and Eve is in some ways a fortunate one, that their sin is the necessary step to their salvation.

But if we are fully aware of this rhythmic pattern of light and darkness, upward and downward movements—of the mythic rather than the logical aspects of Christianity in this poem—we will find something more than a fortunate fall. The paradox of a happy accident is, as A. O. Lovejoy pointed out in his classic paper on "Milton and the Paradox of the Fortunate Fall," part of Christian theology.[1] In terms of the Christian myth, however, the rhythmic pattern that is being described here, the fact that the Fall can bring about a greater happiness, is not a paradox but a part of the natural development of this pattern. The greater good that is revealed to Adam at the end of the poem, "the paradise within" that can be obtained by sinful man, is not an unforeseen accident but is inherent in the very nature of the fall.

For the sinful actions that we are about to witness in Book IX are not caused by Adam or Eve choosing evil when they should have chosen the good. They have no real choice. What they do is part of that pattern, which we have traced in the preceding chapter, in which the exercise of the best qualities bring about evil while the evil consequences bring about good. The disobedience of both Eve and Adam stems from impulses which are inherent in their nature, but which are in conflict with their state of innocence. Both forces, those pulling them forward towards experience and those keeping them in a state of innocence, are equally strong. It is the tension between these forces that can be felt throughout this Book.

When Eve asks for permission to work alone, Adam's first impulse is to agree with her:

> But if much convérse perhaps
> Thee satiate, to short absence I could yield.
> For solitude sometimes is best society
> And short retirement urges sweet return. (247–50)

But his reason for refusing her request is equally convincing. The need for obedience is as strong as the need for freedom;

and Adam's self-esteem, as he was warned, should be as strong as
his susceptibility to Eve's beauty:

> The wife, when danger or dishonor lurks
> Safest and seemliest by her husband stays,
> Who guards her, or with her the worst endures. (267–69)

The soundness of this second argument does not negate the
force of the first one. We are not to decide which is right, but to
recognize that either path, Eve's obedience or her freedom,
would necessitate the loss of something intrinsically valuable.

The theologian (or the narrator in the poem) may decide
that freedom should be subordinated to safety and obedience.
The liberal humanist or modern Christian might very well
agree with Eve; she does after all, as the colloquy continues,
express some of the views in Milton's own *Areopagitica*. But all
of these judgments are, in a sense, extra-literary judgments.
Within the imaginative experience of the poem there is no need
to judge, but to see that both freedom and obedience are both
deeply felt and irreconcilable. It is this feeling that is expressed
by Eve when she asks how God who created a perfect state could
allow such a conflict. And since she believes that God's ways
are perfectly comprehensible to human reason, she is sure that
this contradiction does not exist:

> Let us not then suppose our happy state
> Left so imperfect by the Maker wise
> As not to secure to single or combined.
> Frail is our happiness if this be so,
> And Eden were no Eden thus exposed. (337–41)

Eve is, of course both wrong and right. God did intend that she
remain beside Adam, as the subsequent actions will reveal. But
Eve is right in sensing that their happiness is frail, or at least
extremely vulnerable. Eden in the sense of a perfect state of
innocence does not exist. What we have in the poem is an Eden
that is continually changing and developing.

For unlike traditional gardens, Milton's Paradise is not at all
static, as Barbara Lewalski tells us in a recent essay: "In *Paradise Lost* the Edenic life is radical growth and process, a mode

of life steadily increasing in complexity and challenge and difficulty, but at the same time and by that very fact, in perfection."
And this "perfection" is gained "through ever increasing knowledge and experience."[2] "Perfection" is a paradoxical word in this context, since it traditionally denoted a state of rest, and probably had this Aristotelian connotation for Milton. But, in any case, a life that is "steadily increasing in complexity and challenge and difficulty" is a life that is moving towards the fulfillment of its potentialities. And these potentialities lead from love to passion, from a delight in knowledge to knowing too much; in short, from innocence to experience. Eden is in danger of being lost, is in fact moving towards its disappearance, from the moment of its creation. The very forces that God created in man: the freedom of the will, the sense of plenitude, the intense love between man and woman, the delight in knowledge—all these forces are in conflict with a static world. And there is no question which is stronger.

This movement towards experience can be seen in Adam's final reply to Eve. Strongly as he wants to keep Eve by his side, his own conception of the world leads him to the emphasis on free will: "God left free the will." He modifies this phrase by showing the limits of this freedom and by insisting that Eve show her love for him by being obedient. But after saying all that he can in favor of her remaining with him, the value of freedom comes to the surface again. Eve must make her own decision, even if that decision goes against his will:

> But if thou think trial unsought may find
> Us both securer than thus warned than seem'st.
> Go; for thy stay, not free, absents thee more;
> Go in thy native innocence, rely
> On what thou hast of virtue, summon all,
> For God towards thee hath done his part, do thine. (370–75)

If we look at the events immediately following this advice, we could say that Adam was wrong, and that he should have, as Eve reminds him later, commanded her "absolutely not to go." But clearly such a command would be in opposition to the entire movement of the poem. For God not only gave Adam a command, through Raphael, to be the head; God also created a world in which the freedom of the will is the basis of all human action. It is also, as we have seen, a world in which everything is moving towards the fulfillment of all of its potentialities, evil as well as good. And, most significantly, it is a universe in which (as we have seen in the preceding chapter) good and evil are so interdependent that we cannot have one without the other. Satan must escape from Hell and enter Eden so that out of all his evil there may be greater good. And Eve must, in the same pattern, taste the apple not only that she may fall from inno- cence but so that she may attain grace.

But to agree that Eve must leave and that Adam must allow her to leave, or at least allow her to make her own decision, does not imply approval of their actions. If their decision cannot, as we have argued, be considered wrong, it cannot be considered right either. We are not to judge Adam and Eve at all; to be caught up in the rhythmical pattern of the scene requires that we see their actions as inherent in the contradictions that are built into their situation. If we are looking for an action on the part of Adam or of Eve which would be *right*, which would preserve their Eden and be consistent with their freedom, we are misreading the poem. The tragic quality that gives this scene the greatness that all readers have felt lies in the fact that there is no right answer that Adam could have given.

Adam wants very much to believe (as does Milton) that "best are all things as the will/Of God ordained them" (343–44). But this statement is an expression of his faith in God's ways rather than a description of what we see before us. What we see in the poem is a perfect state in which the exercise of the best impulses in man leads to the loss of this perfection. Once we accept this paradox, we will have no problem in the follow- ing scene. For as Satan tries to seduce Eve into eating the apple, we are witnessing the inevitable realization of all of the possibil- ities that are in Eve.

It is difficult to believe, Satan tells Eve in the next scene, that a just and wise God would "incense his ire/For such a petty trespass," or forbid any knowledge to mankind whom He created in His own image:

> Or will God incense his ire
> For such a petty trespass, and not praise

Rather your dauntless virtue, whom the pain
Of death denounced, whatever thing death be,
Deterred not from achieving what might lead
To happier life, knowledge of good and evil
. . . .
God therefore cannot hurt ye, and be just;
Not just, not God, not feared then or obeyed:
(692–98, 700–701)

To try to find weaknesses in Satan's argument, as many scholars
have done, is easy; but it is beside the point. For Satan's plea is
meant to be strong, and not only to Eve. Its strength lies in the
very nature of Milton's universe that strives to realize all of its
possibilities. In following Satan's invitation, Eve is exercising to
the utmost all the potentialities that God has given her. That
she is punished for her action, that eating the apple leads to the
loss of Paradise, is quite true; and this loss should be felt as
painful:

Earth felt the wound, and Nature from her seat
Sighing through all her works gave signs of woe,
That all was lost. (782–84)

But the pain that we feel, the pain that is produced by the
poetic action, is not caused by Eve's making the wrong choice
but by the stubborn fact that there was no right choice. To try
to condemn Eve or to justify her would, as Helen Gardner has
warned us, destroy the tragic feeling that belongs to the poem.
"As spectators of tragedy we are released from our perpetual
burden of asking ourselves what we ought to do. To use tragedy
either as a moral example or as a moral warning is to destroy
the glory of tragedy. . . ."[3]
   This sense of tragedy brought about by a situation in which
even the best possible action results in a painful loss is even
more emphatic in the next scene, when Adam must choose
between his love for Eve and his obedience to God. Most critics
are more sympathetic to Adam at this point than they are to
Eve. And only those critics who read the poem as a moral
warning are satisfied by a simple condemnation of Adam. Most

critics confess their own sympathy and admiration for the loyalty and the natural passion expressed by Adam, and are troubled by the demand made by the narrator of the poem that we condemn him. How can we condemn a man for wishing to remain with his wife even in death?

> However, I with thee have fixed my lot,
> Certain to undergo like doom: if death
> Consort with thee, death is to me as life;
> So forcible within my heart I feel
> The bond of nature draw me to my own . . . (953–57)

My answer is that we are not being asked to condemn Adam at this point, or to praise him for daring to show his natural feelings even when they lead to disobedience of God. We are asked, I believe, to go beyond praise or blame and sense the tragic irony of this scene: namely, that in giving expression to the most noble feeling that he is capable of, Adam is falling into sin. To be "imparadised in one another's arms," to return to the earlier phrase, is the most certain way of losing Paradise.

Nothing that Adam could do at this moment, obviously, would satisfy both his duty to God and the unbreakable link that binds him to Eve. That God created such an irreconcilable conflict makes us feel that His ways, however justifiable they may be in theology, are not our ways. Judging by the response of numerous readers and critics to this scene, there is no point where the injustice of God seems more striking. Yet at this very point, in conformity with the rhythmic pattern of the entire poem, we are beginning to move towards a justification, in purely human terms, of God's mysterious ways. We do so because the paradox—that even the noblest impulses can lead to sin—can be reversed. If the sin, the loss of innocence, is brought about, in part, by these noble impulses, the sin cannot be entirely evil. The fortunate fall, the *felix culpa* of the theologians as mentioned previously, can be applied here because of the final consequences of the sin. But in relationship to the pattern of the poem itself, *the sin has a fortunate aspect not only in its consequences but in its very nature.* As we look closely at the drama of this scene, and the one immediately following, we can find not only pain and disappointment, but the fulfillment of potentialities in Adam and Eve that were not possible in their state of innocence.

This statement seems to be contradicted by the immediate consequences of the act. As soon as Adam tastes of the forbidden fruit, he looks on Eve with lascivious eyes. The love for Eve, which a few minutes before was a sign of his deepest spiritual qualities—the love that was stronger than death—is now turned to lust. And as they both burn in lust, we see the disappearance of their innocent sexuality. But even at this painful moment, Milton is preparing us for a new relationship that will surpass their former innocent sexuality in range and intensity, as well as in pain. The intensity can be seen immediately, as, with inflamed senses, Adam leads Eve "whose eye darted contagious fire"

>   to a shady bank,
> Thick overhead with verdant roof embow'red
> He led her nothing loth; flowers were the couch,
> Pansies, and violets and asphodel,
> And hyacinth, earth's freshest softest lap. (1036–41)

Their love is of course a guilty love; but Milton does not allow us to forget its beauty, as he lingers over the flowers, reminiscent of the "flow'ry roof" which decorated their marriage bower in Book IV. It is true Adam's remarks, after they awaken, express nothing but regret for the loss of the innocent relationship:

> O Eve, in evil hour thou didst give ear
> To that false worm, of whomsoever taught
> To counterfeit man's voice, true in our fall,
> False in our promised rising; since our eyes
> Opened we find indeed, and find we know
> Both good and evil, good lost and evil got. . . . (1067–72)

But again the reader should be able to see more than Adam. Painful as the knowledge of evil may be for him at this moment, we should also realize that the good requires the evil, that the fulfillment of the potentialities in man, as well as in all of God's creation, requires that Eden be lost. Of course Adam can-

not realize this, anymore than Satan can realize that his efforts
to bring evil out of good only serve to bring about an even
greater good. But the subsequent events in Book X make clear
that knowledge and experience—by bringing Adam and Eve to
great suffering—will also enable them to experience a greater
intimacy, both with each other and with God.

The dramatic significance of the poem is lost if we engage in
a debate about what Adam should have done in Book IX, or
what we would have done in his place, or what the 17th-century
reader would have wanted Adam to have done. Within the
poem, we should be concerned not with our morality but with
the way in which the action here is related to the structure of
the poem. If we do so, we will see that the actions of Adam
develop the interdependence of good and evil that we have
traced throughout the poem. The deepest love of Adam for Eve,
the love that brought them into a perfect union of mind and
body, is the same love that brings them here to lust and
estrangement. At the same time, this lust and estrangement is
the basis for a more intense, exciting and more intimate union
than was ever enjoyed before their fall. To see this final turn of
the paradox, we must go on to Book X.

The quarrel between God and man, and between God and
Satan, which occupies the greater part of this book, will be
discussed later. We will proceed directly to the quarrel between
Adam and Eve, which is even more intense now than when we
left them "in mutual accusation" at the end of Book IX. Adam
now realizes all of the consequences of the fall; and the "Soft
words" uttered by a desolate Eve only inspire greater bitterness
in him:

> Out of my sight, thou serpent! that name best
> Befits thee with him leagued, thyself as false
> And hateful . . .
>
>   But for thee
> I had persisted happy . . .
>
>   O why did God,
> Creator wise, that peopled highest heav'n
> With Spirits masculine, create at last
> This novelty on earth, this fair defect

Of nature, and not fill the earth at once
With men as angels without feminine,
Or find some other way to generate
Mankind? (867–69, 873–74, 888–95)

The very passion that united him to Eve, the "bond of nature" that drew Adam to his wife in the face of death itself, is now regarded as a curse. In the same way, the frank sexuality which, as an immediate consequence of the fall, brought them together in a more intense union, has now caused Adam to find the very sight of Eve hateful. Yet through all of his vituperation, Adam reveals a complete intimacy with Eve, an intimacy in which even the worst feelings are being shared.

There may be hatred for Eve in this long speech, but it is not the hatred that dissolves the bond between them, but the hatred that, by uniting their worst feelings as well as their best, creates an even stronger bond. The tree of knowledge gives them a knowledge of evil, but it is a deeper knowledge all the same. And through this knowledge we can find a realization of greater and more interesting potentialities than could ever be revealed in the state of innocence. This side of the emotion is expressed immediately following Adam's curse on all women.

He added not, and from her turned, but Eve
Not so repulsed, with tears that ceased not flowing,
And tresses all disordered, at his feet
Fell humble, and embracing them, besought
His peace. . . .　　　　　　　　　　(909–13)

The poignancy of this scene has often been noted; and Helen Gardner has reminded us that despite his doctrine of woman's inherent inferiority to man, Milton "in his actual presentation gives Eve the advantage in moral and spiritual qualities." Instead of being repulsed by Adam's cruel speech, Eve reveals "her impulsive generosity in wishing to take all the punishment. . . . As she seeks him in tears and persistence for having sinned against him, she shows him the way by which they may both find pardon. . . ."[4]

In terms of the interpretation presented here, Eve does much more than show Adam the way towards a pardon. She reveals that the bitterness which Adam has expressed towards her, and towards all women, can lead to a greater intimacy between them. Just as the estrangement was caused indirectly, by Adam's intense love for Eve, so the result of this estrangement is an equally noble love for Adam. For Eve also is willing to lose her life by taking upon herself all of the consequences of the sin. Her feelings at this point recall Adam's feelings before eating the apple:

> Forlorn of thee,
> Whither shall I betake me, where subsist?
> . . . .
> Both have sinned, but thou
> Against God only, I against God and thee,
> And to the place of judgment will return,
> There with my cries importune Heaven, that all
> The sentence from thy head removed may light
> On me, sole cause to thee of all this woe. . . . . (921–22, 930–35)

We too are returned, metaphorically, to the "place of judgment," and see the paradoxical justice in Eve's becoming the instrument of their reconciliation. The original scene, stemming as it did from both the best and the worst impulses of both the man and the woman, has its final result in an awakening of a deeper relationship between them.

This deeper and more intense relationship is not necessarily a better one. Nothing that is said and done here can erase the loss of their innocent love. But being joined to each other in sorrow does add another dimension to their love, just as knowing each other (in both senses of the word) at their worst as well as at their best, gives them a more complete intimacy than they could experience before the fall. It is not that their fault was a happy one, or even that it had fortunate consequences; the complete action described in Books IX and X goes beyond our normal categories of happiness and sadness, good and evil, and shows their interdependence. It is here particularly that the myth goes deeper than our morality.

For the evil in this scene, as we have seen previously in the actions of Satan, is the fulfillment of potentialities inherent in the good. The innocent state of Adam and Eve thus requires

that the innocence be lost; for the free will that God gave to
Adam and Eve is fully realized in their disobedience. But this
disobedience, although it results in the loss of Eden, also brings
about the possibility of a "paradise within . . . happier far."
This possibility is made explicit by Michael only at the end of
the poem. But we can feel its reality even now, precisely at the
point where the loss of the external paradise is felt most intense-
ly. Even Anne Ferry who, as we noted before, stresses the sharp
difference between the innocent world and the fallen world,
recognizes that the disorder and conflict in the fallen world
with "its color and movement, excitement and energy" is in
some ways preferable to "the world of unfallen Adam, so fresh
and untroubled and unchanging."[5]

Eve's tears of contrition melt the anger of Adam, who re-
sponds by an equally gallant offer to take all the guilt upon
himself. Eve then suggests that they both go forth eagerly to
accept their punishment of death. But Adam prevails upon her
to accept their punishment as having the possibilities of a
greater good. The pains of childbirth are "soon recompensed
with joy/Fruit of the womb" (1052–53); and we see how the
"fruit" of the forbidden tree brings not only death but also life
into the world. The penalty of labor will enable them with
God's grace

> To pass commodiously this life, sustained
> By him with many comforts, till we end
> In dust, our final rest and native home. (1083–85)

The ambivalence in these lines, the sense of completion and the
sense of loss, can be found in the entire scene. We are made to
find comfort in the results of sin and at the same time feel the
pain as well as the inevitability in the loss of innocence. The
obedience of Adam and Eve has now brought about an acceptance of God's ways that goes beyond the acceptance that occurred before the fall. God's actions before the fall were revealed to them in a world of eternal delight. Now God's actions
produce pain and death, and to mankind this punishment must
seem unjust. Therefore, to obey and worship God now reveals a
deeper understanding of Him on the part of Adam and Eve

than they could ever have attained in the state of innocence. As they water the ground with their penitent tears, they seem closer to God and to each other than they have ever been before. But their closeness to God also involves a separation from Him. We can see the full implications of this paradox by turning to the opening scene of this Book, in which God sends His own Son both to judge man and to suffer for man's sin.

God's opening speech, as almost all of His speeches, is a defense of His allowing evil to be set loose in the world. Again, as in Book III, God insists that although He predicted Satan's success, man alone is morally responsible for the fall: "no decree of mine" could interfere with man's "free will." There is of course no overt rebuttal on the part of the Son who announces that he will go down to the earth to deliver judgment on the fallen pair. At the same time, however, there is an implicit indication that God too is partly responsible for the sin. For Christ also announces that he will eventually pay for man's sin, that the "worst on me must light." We are also told that the crucifixion will "mitigate their doom." But these oblique references do not really bring in the crucifixion. The avoidance of this subject is an interesting aspect of Milton's whole conception of Christianity; and no doubt Milton was always insistent on the individual taking full responsibility for his guilt. But in this context there is, I believe, a special significance in emphasizing Christ's role as a messenger of God rather than as the sacrificial lamb.

For too strong a reminder of the crucifixion might suggest that God is aware, despite His heated denials, of some responsibility for man's fall. To offer up His only begotten Son might suggest that God is making some atonement for His crime in permitting Satan to enter the garden. But any admission, even indirectly, of God's responsibility for the fall would not fit into the context of this scene. Adam, as we shall soon see, may blame God for man's plight. But the narrator cannot. The whole doctrinal force of the poem lies in its justification of God; and the references to the earthly role of Christ are so oblique as to avoid any suggestion of Christ's death as an atonement. Man alone must atone for his sins, and the judgment proceeds with little interruption. There is a brief attempt on Adam's part to blame God. In admitting Eve's role in offering him the apple, Adam reminds God that Eve was given to him as God's

> perfect gift, so good
> So fit, so acceptable, so divine
> That from her hand I could suspect no ill,
> And what she did, whatever in itself,
> Her doing seemed to justify the deed;
> She gave me of the tree and I did eat.   (138–43)

But Adam is quickly silenced by Christ's question, "Was she thy God, that her thou didst obey." It is only when he is alone that the human objection to the divine viewpoint is expressed by Adam. But when it does come, its force is great. What Adam could not say in the presence of Christ, he can say when he is alone. After the long scene taken up with Satan's return to Hell, and the ambivalent triumph of Sin and Death, we find Adam lamenting his fate. His speech is very long (720–844) and is marked by both a diatribe against God and, at the same time, an acceptance of his fate. The questioning of God's justice, however, is the dominant theme:

> O fleeting joys
> Of Paradise, dear bought with lasting woes!
> Did I request thee, Maker, from my clay
> To mold me man, did I solicit thee
> From darkness to promote me, or here place
> In this delicious garden?   (741–46)

Even when he grants that the maker has a right to reduce his creation back to dust, Adam still asks why death was not

> Sufficient penalty, why hast thou added
> The sense of endless woes? Inexplicable
> Thy justice seems. . . .   (752–55)

It is true that after this outcry about God's justice being "inexplicable," Adam concludes that "his doom is fair." But this phrase is only a temporary stopping point in the condemnation of God. For Adam goes on to question why God's judgment

must be inflicted on their innocent progeny. Why cannot Adam
alone suffer for the sin that he alone committed?

> Ah! why should all mankind
> For one man's fault thus guiltless be condemned,
> If guiltless. But from me what can proceed
> But all corrupt, both mind and will depraved,
> Not to do only, but to will the same
> With me?   (822-27)

The answer is clear. The payment for the sin of Adam must
descend through all the generations of man. And Adam tells us
that this decree of God is nevertheless just: "Him after all
disputes/Forced I absolve." (828-29)

The reader may still question whether God is logically "ab-
solved," whether God is still not responsible for a decree which
is cruel according to the human standards that Adam invokes.
There is nothing in the soliloquy that indicates Adam's satisfaction with God's actions. Of course Adam strives desperately and
sincerely to place the blame on himself:

> All my evasions vain.
> And reasonings, though through mazes, lead me still
> But to my own conviction: first and last
> On me, me only, as the source and spring
> Of all corruption, all the blame lights due. . . . (829-33)

But the attempt is not completely successful. As Marjorie Nicolson has said, "Adam has been rationalizing, intellectualizing
with his 'discursive reason.' He acknowledges justice with his
mind, but does not *feel* it in his heart. Indeed his despair is
even more profound at the end of his speech than it was when
he began by saying 'O miserable of Happy!' " Miss Nicolson
then quotes his last sentence to indicate "that he has found no
comfort."[6]

> O conscience! into what abyss of fears
> And horrors hast thou driv'n me; out of which
> I find no way, from deep to deeper plunged! (842-44)

I would go further and say that Adam is not even convinced

intellectually of God's justice. All that we can see in his "rationalizing" is the strong desire to be convinced, perhaps a desperate need to be convinced, not the conviction itself. We can better account for the extreme agitation of this soliloquy (indicated by the jagged rhythms and the difficult syntax) by assuming that Adam, like Milton's readers, cannot understand why a just God acts as He does.

At this point we can see in a brief compass the relationship between dogma and poetry that we have been tracing throughout the poem. The dogma is certainly here: "his doom is fair," and "On me, me only . . . all the blame lights due." But in the context of the entire speech and in the context of the actions that preceded the speech, this statement is not so much a defense of God's fairness as a statement of Adam's need to assume a just God. The need is a strong one, as no doubt it was in Milton. But the obstacles to such a belief, the inexplicability of God's justice, is equally strong. The tension that is generated by this conflict, not the validity of either side of the argument, is what lies at the emotional center of the poem. It is the honest description of the struggle between two strong forces that gives the poem its literary power, and transforms an argument about dogma into poetry.

My emphasis on the inexplicability of God's justice may seem strange in a work devoted to justifying the ways of God to man. But it is precisely this element of recalcitrance, the power of experience to escape the intellectual pattern set for it by the author, that is basic to dramatic tension, wherever we find it. What Dorothy Walsh has to say about dramatic tension in general terms has a particular relevance to *Paradise Lost*: "We cannot hope for intelligibility unless we have order, but the order of impressive works of literature in the mode of dramatic tension is an order in which some element of the inexplicable, of the recalcitrant, of the obdurate, of the unmanageable, is preserved and makes itself felt."[7]

In *Paradise Lost*, the emotions of Adam and Eve are, of course, obdurate and recalcitrant. But these emotions contribute to the order and intelligibility of the poem. For what causes Adam's redemption is not logic, but, appropriately enough in this context, a strong emotion. It is not an understanding of God's ways but a response to Eve's love that turns Adam from despair to the path of regeneration. As many readers have already noted, the emotional attachment to Eve which had brought about his falling away from God is now the direct cause of Adam's return to God. And Eve brings Adam back to God, not by logic, but by an appeal to his emotions. The triumph of his emotions over his reason, which had caused Adam to eat the apple, is now the first step towards that "paradise within," which will be promised by Michael in the conclusion. Before he can be genuinely reconciled to God, Adam must first be reconciled to Eve. The love that seemed to have destroyed them is now the means to their salvation.

As a final turn of the screw, this love for Eve is prefixed by hatred. In response to her entreaties, Adam's reply is "Out of my sight, thou serpent." But as we have seen in our discussion of this scene, the hatred itself is not altogether destructive. It clears the air and brings the couple closer to each other than ever before.

The main argument of this chapter can be summarized more easily by first placing the events in Books IX and X in a chronological perspective: We first see Adam and Eve argue as to whether she should face Satan alone, and they arrive at the decision that her freedom was worth the risk of danger. Confronted with Satan's invitation to eat the apple, Eve reveals that her desire for knowledge and freedom, as well as for equality with Adam, are stronger than her fear of God or her obedience to Adam. After eating the apple, Eve's egotism is intensified; but she offers to share the fruit with Adam out of love for him as well as out of jealousy. Overcome by his love for Eve, Adam eats the forbidden fruit and they both discover lust. Their greater intimacy brings hatred and separation between them, just as their greater knowledge separates them from God. Adam accepts the judgment of Christ; but his punishment brings him to complete despair. Only Eve's tears bring Adam back to her and to God.

In each of these incidents the full exercise of the impulses in man leads to evil; and the evil, as it becomes fully realized, brings about a greater good. Thus good and evil become interdependent. They remain opposite forces; but as two opposite poles they attract rather than repel each other. Obedience and

disobedience, love and lust, free will and determinism, innocence and sin, follow so close upon each other that it is difficult
to believe that we can have one without the other. Milton's
universe, or the universe of Milton's God, seems to demand the
full realization of all of its potentialities.

But such a universe comes into conflict with the expressed
doctrines of the narrator who, time and again, insists on a sharp
separation between good and evil, innocence and experience,
reason and feeling. The narrator also insists that there is a
rational pattern to the events, and that this pattern is consistent
with human justice. And Milton himself may very well have
wanted "to control and categorize experience . . . and to comprehend it intellectually," as one critic has stated.[8] But the poem
goes beyond the intention of the narrator, and perhaps beyond
even Milton's own conscious intentions. For what is presented to
us is more than an experience that is cut and fitted to a set
of moral doctrines. The need to accept God's ways and to fit
them into our own concepts of justice is balanced with the frank
recognition that His ways are not ours. And it is the dramatic tension between the need for acceptance and the urge to
question, the rational order and the stubborn intractability of
experience, that gives the poem its emotional center—and accounts for its enduring power as poetry.

Such a reading is, of course, incomplete, in many ways. But if
we accept this duality in the rhythmic pattern as central to the
action, we can respond to the poem without reference to our
moral presuppositions. Our moral feelings are engaged, as were
Milton's. Certainly reading these two books involved our feelings about obedience and rebellion, sexuality and restraint, belief in God's goodness as well as disbelief. But our feelings, if
this reading accomplished its purpose, were absorbed in the
poetic experience, in the tragic irony of the action, just as
Milton's religious feelings were absorbed by the intractable
myth. To read literature without an ideology (or to write it)
does not imply any loss of strong moral convictions. Surely John
Milton would be the last poet to be accused of any such lack.
But both the writing and the reading of great literature does
involve a capacity for going beyond our personal feelings in
order to enter into another kind of experience. However we

define this aesthetic experience, its value must surely lie in its difference from, as well as in its resemblance to, our emotions in everyday experience. And it is this difference between what is already present in the Christian doctrines and what is created by the poem that lies at the center of our imaginative experience.

NOTES

1. "Milton and the Paradox of the Fortunate Fall," *Essays in the History of Ideas* (Baltimore, 1948), pp. 277–95.
2. "Innocence and Experience in Milton's Eden," *New Essays on Paradise Lost,* ed. Thomas Kranidas (Berkeley and Los Angeles, 1969), pp. 88, 100.
3. *A Reading of Paradise Lost* (Toronto, 1965), p. 118.
4. Ibid., pp. 87–88.
5. *Milton's Epic Voice* (Cambridge, Mass., 1963), p. 81.
6. Marjorie Nicolson, *John Milton, A Readers Guide to His Poetry* (New York, 1963), p. 303.
7. *Literature and Knowledge* (Middletown, Conn., 1969), p. 70.
8. J. B. Broadbent, "Milton's 'Mortal Voice' and his 'Omnific Word.'" In *Approaches To Paradise Lost,* ed. C. A. Patrides (London, 1968), p. 117.

VI

The Reader's Attitude
in *Paradise Regained*

UNLIKE ITS GREAT predecessor, *Paradise Regained* has not brought about any sharp controversies among its critics concerning its theme. There is general agreement that Christ's victory over Satan is a victory for the unseen kingdom of heaven over the kingdoms of this world, and that Christ achieves this victory not by acting but as one critic has phrased it, "by a special kind of not-acting, by a special kind of conquering weakness, 'By Humiliation and strong sufferance'."[1] But this very decisiveness and lack of self-doubt in the hero of the poem has created its own problems for the critics. How can a poem generate suspense, or any kind of excitement, when the issue is so clear and the outcome so inevitable? Closely connected with this question is the question of the reader's attitude toward this perfect hero. Can the reader really identify and sympathize with a hero who rejects without a struggle the beauty and the glory of the only world that he knows? And even if we grant that Christ by his very nature must reject this world, we can still ask, as a recent critic has done, why Milton cannot describe this rejection, the negation of the world offered by Satan, with the same imaginative force that he describes the temptations. "Imaginative temptations should be met imaginatively."[2]

Milton scholars have been aware of these questions and have made great efforts to justify the high regard that they have for this poem. In particular, the scholars have tried to justify the seemingly harsh, ascetic attitude of Christ. Antecedents for the Christ of *Paradise Regained* have been found in literary as well as in religious traditions. His attitudes and values have been traced to classical, medieval, and renaissance sources, as well as

75

to earlier stages of Milton's own life. And some critics have tried
to reconcile the ascetic values exemplified by Christ with the
values of secular and humanist traditions in the present and
in the past.[3] Much of this scholarship is convincing on its own
terms; and even when it is not convincing, the critics have often
enabled us to see many aspects of the work that are generally
unnoticed. My disagreement is not with the results of the scholarship but with an assumption that lies behind it. The assump-,
tion that I intend to question is that the success of the poem
depends on the reader's ability to sympathize and agree with
Christ's actions, and conversely, that the reader must be repelled
by Satan and by the temptations that Satan offers. I hope to
show that these assumptions are unnecessary, and that our disagreement and lack of sympathy for Christ, far from being an
obstacle to our appreciation, is the main source of the tension
that gives the poem its dramatic interest.

The belief that we must sympathize with Christ is made most
explicit by W. W. Robson: "the success of the poem depends
on the reader's willingness to imagine himself in sympathy with
certain religious and ethical doctrines. . . . And a fair criticism of
the poem here is that Milton, by his presentation of Christ, has
done something to disturb that sympathy where it already exists,
and to hinder its attainment where it does not."[4] The same
assumptions can also be found in a leading defender of the
poem, Arnold Stein. After admitting that the temptations
offered by Satan "make very good sense as we very well know,"
Stein insists that "it is the business of the poem to convince us
that in the drama the sense is an absolutely wrong sense."[5] He
does qualify this statement by adding that the poem must "convince us as a poem" and not, presumably, as an argument. But
the distinction is not made very clear.

The point of view presented here comes closer to that of
Northrop Frye in that he believes that the reader's feelings are
necessarily at variance with the feelings of the hero. "All of us
are like Christ in the world, and unlike him, partly of it.
Whatever in us is of the world is bound to condemn Christ's
rejection of the world at some point or other."[6] But this condemnation of Christ, Frye maintains, exists only on the dramatic
level; and he implies that "the conceptual aspects of the

situation" require us to regard Christ as a perfect hero. In my reading of the poem there is no need to choose between the conceptual or dramatic. Neither the correctness of Milton's theology nor the natural responses of the reader to an almost inhuman Christ has to be sacrificed or explained away. On the contrary, the contrast between our feelings, our human desires for the glories of this world, and the rejection of these desires by Christ is the emotional center of this poem.

As Christ comes to a realization of his true identity, that he is divine and not merely human, he must give up part of his humanity. And the reader, of course, is made to understand just why this must be done. But the reader cannot, no matter how much he understands, give up his humanity also. Milton does not allow the reader to do so, because the temptations of Satan are described in such a way as to reveal their attractive force. Even the young Christ is tempted by the hopes of redeeming this world by human actions. We are constantly reminded that Christ is a fusion of the human as well as of the divine. He is at all times a God–Man, subject, at least potentially, to human temptations.[7] In his first soliloquy Christ recounts how inspired he was by his hope of driving out evil from this world so that "truth" could be "freed, and equity restored." To do this work, he had at first put his trust in precisely those forces which Satan will soon tempt him with, more military and political power: .

> Victorious deeds
> Flamed in my heart, heroic acts: one while
> To rescue Israel from the Roman yoke,
> Then to subdue and quell o'er all the earth
> Brute violence and proud tyrannic pow'r,
> Till truth were freed, and equity restored.
> Yet held it more humane, more heavenly, first
> By winning words to conquer willing hearts,
> And make persuasions do the work of fear. (I. 215–23)

The obvious contrast here is between the martial deeds and persuasion by "willing words." Christ has no difficulty in giving up his dreams of military glory. But what is significant for the future development of the poem is that the military spirit pervades the entire passage. Even the "persuasion" is linked to the "heroic acts" on the battlefield by such expressions as "conquer," "fear," and "to subdue." Of course, what Milton wants to do is to make clear that in forsaking the traditional role of a hero, Christ is not forsaking his active role. He means to be just as active in his withdrawal from this world as he would be if he were in the world. But the poet cannot (nor, I believe did he intend to) prevent us from associating such words as "conquer" and "subdue" with the martial valor described so vividly in the first part of this passage. As a result, the active military life in the literal sense, the life soon to be offered by Satan, is not so much rejected by Christ as raised to a higher level. The picture of Christ who wants to wield words like weapons should be in our minds as we come to the first temptation.

Also present in our minds as we come to the actual temptations should be the Old Testament tradition of a Messiah that has been described by Christ in the preceding passage. Northrop Frye makes a specific analogy between Christ and Moses whose "deliverance of Israel from Egypt prefigures his (Christ's) life in the Gospels. Israel is led to Egypt by a Joseph; Christ is taken from Israel by a Joseph. . . . The Israelites conquer the Promised Land under Joshua who has the same name as Jesus."[8] What is significant for our purposes at this point is the active, military role that the recollection of Moses and Joshua brings to our mind, and, in turn, reinforces Christ's references to the "victorious deeds" that "flamed" in his heart. This military note is strengthened even further by the similarity, noted by a number of scholars, between Milton's Christ and Spenser's Guyon. For Guyon and the Red Cross Knight in *The Faerie Queene* were examples of a long medieval tradition of the Christ–Knight who actively destroys the evil in this world. In view of the many associations with military prowess, we can see that the passive, negative attitude that Christ will express in response to Satan's temptations comes into opposition not only with Satan but also with active values that are part of the Christian tradition. That Christ in this poem turns away from these values without hesitation does not mean that the reader must be equally indifferent to them, as we see in the first temptation:

> But if thou be the Son of God, command
> That out of these hard stones be made thee bread;

So shalt thou save thyself and us relieve
With food, whereof we wretched seldom taste. (I. 342-45)

Christ's answer is clear and his victory over Satan seems to be complete. But looked at more closely the answer does not satisfy either our reason or our emotions. That it was "God who fed our fathers here with manna" does not contradict Satan's request that, as the son of God as well as the successor to Moses, Christ could very well call on God again to "relieve/With food" the hungry. Nor is the historic Christ above performing miracles. Christ came out of the wilderness "to heal the broken-hearted, to preach deliverance to the captives, and recovery of sight to the blind." (Luke XVIII) In a theological sense we can understand, of course, that the Christ who set out to redeem this world, the Christ who healed the sick and who drove the money changers from the temple, must give way to the Christ who dies for the world in order to usher in a kingdom of heaven. But what we understand theologically is not necessarily accepted emotionally. And in the context of this scene, our natural disappointment that Christ *cannot* feed the hungry, that this good deed, paradoxically, belongs to Satan, is a necessary part of that dramatic struggle that will gradually remove Christ completely from the hopes and desires of ordinary mortals. Christ's heroism is, therefore, not made ineffective, or even weakened, when it encounters resistance on the part of the reader. The resistance is made use of by Milton to bring about the difference between Christ and the ordinary hero, and thus to exalt Christ, to let us see his heroism, in the words of A. S. P. Woodhouse, "as something new and distinctive, different not simply in degree, but in kind from every other."[9]

This distinctive quality of heroism in this poem is, of course, a heroism that is uniquely Christian. It is a heroism that reaches its victory by defeat, its gift of everlasting life by requiring its hero to die a cruel death. And Woodhouse mentions in the same essay that "In *Paradise Regained,* passion in its root sense is the prevailing note."[10] And this sense of active suffering, a willing endurance of hardship and pain, is seen most clearly in Book II, with the speech of Mary. It is not surprising that Milton, who throughout his works has scarcely acknowledged the existence of the mother of Christ, makes use of her at this point. For it is a mother who feels deeply and simply the loss of her son's humanity even as she realizes that he is losing his human ambitions only to gain a heavenly triumph. Her entire speech emphasizes the sense of loss, and thus serves as a contrast to the untroubled, superior attitude of her Son:

> O what avails me now that honor high
> To have conceived of God, or that Salute
> 'Hail, highly favored, among women blest!'
> While I to sorrows am no less advanced. . . . (II. 66–69)

This irrational movement toward glory and sorrow, defeat in triumph, is expressed by Mary when she refers to Simeon's prophecy

> That to the full rising he shall be
> Of many in Israel, and to a sign
> Spoken against, that through my very soul
> A sword shall pierce. . . .   (II. 88–91)

Our knowledge that the crucifixion shall mark Christ's victory over death, and the beginning of our redemption, does not lessen our sympathy with the *Mater dolorosa*, as the sword pierces her soul. Whatever may be true in theology, a literary work does not, at its deepest level, allow one feeling to cancel out another. It is, instead, the fusion of these contrasting feelings that creates the tone or mood. Even when Christ seems to achieve such easy and complete victory over Satan, the sense of loss is still present.

The second temptation is, of course, not really the second, since the temptation of beautiful women is never actually offered to Christ. If Belial's suggestion to "Set women in his eye and in his walk" is not even considered by Satan, why is it included in the poem? No one questions the poet's ability to suggest in a few lines the traditional power of beautiful women. We see this ability not only in the explicitly seductive lines of Belial but also in the rejoinder of Satan, who lingers on the beauty of women even while he denies its power:

> In wood or grove by mossy fountain-side,
> In valley or green meadow, to waylay

Some beauty rare, Callisto, Clymene,
Daphne, or Semele, Antiopa. . . . (II. 184–87)

But what is the purpose of all this if Satan rejects this temptation, since Christ is so far removed from this weakness that it is
never even presented to him? Without attempting to guess just
what Milton may have had in mind, we can see that the effect of
the scene on the reader is closely related to the development
of the entire poem. The natural response of the reader to
the vision of beauty and sexuality reminds him of his delight in
the pleasures of this world. And when we realize that Christ is
completely oblivious to these desires, as the historical Christ
would be, our distance from him is increased. The scene
sharpens our awareness of Christ's non-human qualities and so
reinforces the difference between our feelings and his.

The passage may have another function, even more directly
related to the development of the action. Since it is, interesting-
ly enough, Satan who denounces the power of women, whose
"Beauty stands/In the admiration only of weak minds," and
since this disdain is obviously shared by Christ, we gain increased respect for Satan also.

The banquet set in the wilderness before the hungry Christ,
the immense wealth that is next offered to him, and the military
power (which opens Book III) can all be treated briefly.
For attractive as these temptations may be, there is no further
development in the reactions of either Christ or Satan. It is only
in the last of these scenes that we see the high price that
must be paid for rejecting this world. The necessity of paying
this price is, of course, made convincing by Christ; and the
tension in the poem increases. Satan's offer of military power so
that Christ can become a conquering King of Israel concludes with the appeal:

to free
Thy country from her heathen servitude;
So shalt thou best fulfill, best verify
The Prophets old, who sung thy endless reign. (III. 175–78)

Christ seems to recognize that this promise is indeed part of the

Old Testament, and the acerbic tone of his reply (III. 134–45) gives way to a thoughtful examination of just what Christ can do to replace his Old Testament task. Rather than simply reject his role as a Hebrew Messiah, Christ accepts the role with the qualification that

> All things are best fulfilled in their due time,
> And time there is for all things, Truth hath said.
> If of my reign prophetic Writ hath told
> That it shall never end, so when begin
> The Father in his purpose hath decreed. . . . (III. 182–86)

Northrop Frye has said that the difficulty of Christ throughout the poem "is complicated by the fact that he is still, at this stage of his career, within the law: His temptation is only a part of a much subtler process of separating, in his own mind, the law which is to be annihilated from the law which is to be fulfilled and internalized."[11] At this point we can see how gradual is this process of separation. And even more important, we should recognize that what is offered by Satan is a path of action deeply imbedded in the Old Testament and, consequently, still present in the mind of Christ.

But if our feelings are naturally in sympathy with the Old Testament tradition, we should also understand the special kind of heroism that is required to move into an unknown region where the greatest action is inaction and the highest affirmation of life involves a negation of life as we know it. Few critics would deny either of these feelings. But what is at least implied by most Miltonists is that the first feeling, our impulse to urge Christ to accept the life of action, is wrong, and that we must see that Christ's antipathy for everything that is offered by Satan is right. My point is that the rightness or wrongness of the different paths are of concern only to theology or morality, and that these questions are outside of the poem. Within the poem, we are concerned only with the imaginative experience. On this level the important point is not whether Christ or Satan is right. What is important is to see and to feel the terrible price that must be paid by Christ in order to accomplish a greater triumph than is possible to mortals. And the price is terrible. It involves pain, because as we all know, the Christ who is to accomplish by "deeds above heroic" a divine plan is at the same time a human being like ourselves who will soon meet a cruel death.

The fact that it is Satan who wants to remove this suffering does not make the suffering, the "tribulations, injuries, insults" (III. 190) any less real. Nor does the life of action that Satan advocates even more strongly in the next temptation lose its attractiveness because of the nature of the giver. For at this point, the temptation of Parthia, we see not only a temptation of unusual force, but a tempter who reveals for the first time human qualities that bring him closer to the reader. The temptation itself, a power that would enable Christ to ascend "the throne of David in full glory,/From Egypt to Euphrates and beyond," is described with such vividness and evident delight on the part of the poet that only a long quotation can do this passage justice. (The reader is referred to III. 267–387). But the tempter at the opening of this scene is even more interesting than the temptation. Just after Christ refuses David's crown and before the offer of Parthia, Christ questions his antagonist more sharply than at any point so far. Christ seems to be as curious about the real nature of Satan as Satan is about the nature of Christ. Why does Satan want his glory, Christ asks, "Knows't thou not my rising is thy fall/And my promotion will be thy destruction?" (III. 201–2). Satan's answer is not disappointing. Its emotional depth recalls the Satan of *Paradise Lost*:

> Let that come when it comes; all hope is lost
> Of my reception into grace; what worse?
> For where no hope is left, is left no fear.
> If there be worse, the expectation more
> Of worse torments me than the feeling can.
> I would be at the worst; worst is my port,
> My harbour and my ultimate respose,
> The end I would attain, my final good. (III. 204–11)

The remainder of the speech is equally good; and Milton's rhetorical mastery has been commented upon by many readers. But our interest here is in just how this change in Satan affects the theme. It does so, I believe, because the perceptive analysis

of his own plight gives greater authenticity to the final temptations. We have already noticed how strongly these temptations
appeal to our human inclinations, and even to our highest
values. But in this scene, in which Satan examines his own
position, we are made aware of the human quality of the tempter as well, and his humanity is revealed in such a way as to
identify him with the reader. After facing honestly the reality of
his position, as we have seen in the opening lines, Satan
reveals his need for mercy, even as he realizes his inability to
receive it:

> though to that gentle brow
> Willingly I could fly, and hope thy reign,
> From that placid aspect and meek regard,
> Rather than aggravate my evil state,
> Would stand between me and thy Father's ire. (III. 215–19)

We could, of course, interpret this passage as an act of hypocrisy,
another example of Satan as a deceiver. But such an interpretation, even if it satisfied some theological principle, would
not account for the effect that these lines have on the reader.
And we would then have to assume that Milton in this passage
wrote better than he knew, and was unaware of what effect his
lines would have. It would seem more reasonable to assume that
the poet knew what he was doing, and that he intended to
make Satan appealing at this moment. Milton is also aware, as I
read this passage, of how cruel and insensitive Christ appears to
be. But there is no paradox if we see that throughout the entire
poem Christ progressively rejects those human values and human feelings that prevent him from realizing his divine nature.
That he does so only that he may redeem all humanity is a
paradox in the Christian mystery, but it is perfectly consistent
with the theme of the poem. Just as the readers can admire the
human glories that Christ must reject, so the reader can and
should be sensitive to the pain that Satan experiences. For
Satan's pain is our pain also. This difference between our response and the response of Christ is made even sharper in the
final book.

In the opening temptation of Book IV, Satan presents Christ
with a vision of "glorious Rome, queen of the earth." We are

not surprised, or should not be by this time, at Christ's refusal: "this grandeur and majestic show/of luxury" does not "allure mine eye" (IV. 110–12). The second part of Christ's reply is not surprising either; but the reasons for his rejection are much more coherent than previously offered, and sharpen the division between Christ and the human values of the reader. Christ will indeed redeem man, but in a way far different from the redemption that we would ordinarily expect. For as they are now, men are incapable of being redeemed:

What wise and valiant man would seek to free
These thus degenerate, by themselves enslaved,
Or could of inward slaves make outward free?
Know therefore when my season comes to sit
On David's throne, it shall be like a tree
Spreading and overshadowing all the earth,
Or as a stone that shall to pieces dash
All monarchies besides throughout the world,
And of my kingdom there shall be no end. (IV. 143–51)

It is not only human values but human beings that Christ is turning away from. The evil in the world does not lie in the "tyrannic power" that Christ as a young man had dreamed of subduing by means of "heroic acts" (I. 215–19). The evil lies within man, and no outward action, or no action at all as we usually think of action, can make free the "inward slaves." If we are "degenerates" and by ourselves "enslaved," a much more radical force, indeed a destructive force, must first be let loose before Christ's kingdom can come to pass. And although Christ follows these lines by saying that he cannot now tell just how this kingdom will be attained: ". . . but what the means/Is not for thee to know, or me to tell" (IV. 151–53), we are told in more general terms what these means are. It is clear that our salvation will be something quite different from what salvation would ordinarily mean. Christ will not save us in the same way as Moses, Joshua, or David. And just as the historic Christ was rejected by those who expected him to follow in this Hebrew tradition, so the readers who like all men are more interested in this world than in the next one are also inclined to reject Milton's Christ. Milton is not only describing a historical situation, as some scholars have noted, but re-creating in us those feelings that the historic Christ must have encountered when he moved away from being a son of man to become the Son of God.

Once we understand that Christ must separate himself from us, and that degenerate and inwardly enslaved as we are by the world around us, we cannot be like Christ, we will not be troubled, as so many readers have been, by the great scene of this poem: the rejection of classical learning. Traditional critics who assume that we must share the feelings and values of the hero have always been troubled by Christ's total rejection of all the wisdom and the beauty that belongs to Athens, described in the most memorable lines in the poem:

> Thence to the famous orators repair,
> Those ancient, whose resistless eloquence
> Wielded at will that fierce democraty,
> Shook the Arsenal and fulmined over Greece,
> To Macedon, and Artaxerxes' throne;
> To sage philosophy next lend thine ear,
> From heaven descended to the low-roofed house
> Of Socrates. . . .   (IV. 267–74)

Tillyard, sensitive to the fact that classical learning permeates all of Milton's work, including this very poem, has described the tone of this scene "as one of mortification and masochism."[2] More recent Miltonists have tried to explain this rejection of Athens by showing its continuity with earlier tendencies in Milton. Arnold Stein has attempted to reconcile Christ's attitude with Milton's earlier love for learning by distinguishing the *learning* that is rejected here from the *wisdom* that is still left for us to gain.[13] But no reasoning, however ingenious, can erase the fact that "Athens the eye of Greece, Mother of arts and eloquence" is completely rejected by Christ, and all of its philosophers and poets thrust aside.

To understand this passage in terms of the poem (and not as an outpouring of some hidden guilt or masochistic streak in the poet), we must see it as the final and most dramatic step in Christ's progress: He is now disengaging himself completely from all that is valuable in this world. For a hero who has embraced suffering and humiliation for himself, who has been deaf to the cry for sympathy from the suffering humanity around him, there can be no value in the wisdom of this world. Our sense of loss, as we move away from the vision of Athens, is part of the effect that Milton intended to create. Our separation from Christ should increase as the poem draws to its conclusion, as Christ makes more explicit his own estrangement not only from the desires of humanity, but from all life, even his own. Satan is telling the truth, as usual, when he concludes this scene by predicting Christ's final end on earth:

>   if I read aught in heaven,
> Or heav'n write aught of fate, by what the stars
> Voluminous, or single characters
> In their conjunctions met, give me to spell,
> Sorrows, and labors, opposition, hate,
> Attends thee, scorns, reproaches, injuries,
> Violence and stripes, and lastly cruel death. . . . (IV. 382–88)

But, as usual, Satan's truth is limited to what can be seen in this world. His concluding remarks indicate that he has no real understanding of the fact that the "cruel death" is not the final end of Christ, but the prelude to everlasting life. A truth of this kind cannot be seen in the stars.

> A kingdom they portend thee, but what kingdom,
> Real or allegoric, I discern not,
> Nor when; eternal sure, as without end,
> Without beginning; for no date prefixed
> Directs me in the starry rubric set. (IV. 389–93)

Nor can a kingdom that is removed from space and time, and about which we cannot even use such terms as "real" or "allegoric," be any clearer to our understanding than it is to Satan's. Divine truth is not the same kind of truth as the empirical truth of everyday experience. What Satan says may be only a partial truth, but it is the part that can be seen and felt by ordinary men; his ignorance is ours also. And conversely, Christ's knowl-

edge is knowledge based on an experience that only he can
have. As he goes back into the wilderness for the last time, we
see an anticipation of his death and rebirth.

After rejecting the temptation of Athens, Christ is thrust into
the wilderness by Satan, and a terrible storm arises in the
darkness of the night. Satan then disturbs Christ with "ugly
dreams."

> Ill wast thou shrouded then,
> O patient Son of God, yet only stood'st
> Unshaken; nor yet stayed the terror there:
> Infernal ghosts, and hellish furies, round
> Environed thee; some howled, some yelled, some shrieked,
> Some bent at thee their fiery darts, while thou
> Sat'st unappalled in calm and sinless peace. (IV. 419–25)

Christ's removal from the concerns of worldly men is strengthened by the contrast in this passage between the furious action
of the elements around him and the complete absence of action
by Christ. The lack of motion is suggested by such words as
"patient," "stoods't," "unshaken," and finally, after the howling
and shrieking, the quiet contrast: "thou/Sat'st unappalled in
calm and sinless peace." The raging storm can be seen as an
analogue of Christ's crucifixion and death, as Barbara Lewalski
has pointed out.[14] But it is in the final temptation that Milton
uses most effectively the image of motionlessness to remove
Christ dramatically from the world of action.

It is Satan, of course, who represents worldly action as he
takes the unmoved Christ from the wilderness

> and without wing
> Of hippogrif bore through the air sublime
> Over the wilderness and o'er the plain. . . . (IV. 541–43)

to set him on the "highest pinnacle." Christ is then asked to
prove his divinity by casting himself down from the pinnacle
and being received by the angels. The exact terms of this temptation are not significant; and even if critics are sometimes
puzzled by the precise nature of the temptation, there need be
no problem about the dramatic effect. For the "highest pinnacle"

is a simple but effective image of the fact that Christ has now reached the utmost point in his removal from the world. And his physical response, namely, that he "stood," makes the sharpest possible contrast to the life of action that Satan has been urging throughout the poem. Satan's fall, which follows immediately, represents the final victory of the passive Christ over the active forces of this world. Barbara Lewalski is again very perceptive in linking this scene with the Passion. "The tower episode actualizes the violence threatened and portended in the storm scene, suggesting the crucifixion in which Christ submitted himself to satanic violence and paradoxically, overthrew it by that very submission. In addition to this the tower scene points to Christ's ascension, since it shows Christ's conquest of Satan in his kingdom of the air."[15]

This heavenly triumph as opposed to the worldly triumph that he did not seek is imaged in the next scene in which he is received by the angels

> Who on their plumy vans received him soft
> From his uneasy station, and upbore
> As on a floating couch through the blithe air;
> Then in a flow'ry valley set him down
> On a green bank, and set before him spread
> A table of celestial food, divine. . . . (IV. 583–88)

We should note the continuity as well as the differences between this scene and the preceding temptations. The miraculous fall and the miraculous banquet in the wilderness are precisely what Satan also offered to Christ. Of course, there is an essential difference between the two banquets: What had been offered as temptation by Satan is now accepted by Christ as a reward from God. The fact that the original temptation is transformed into a heavenly gift, however, supports the reader's spontaneous feeling that what Satan offers to Christ is not altogether evil.

By being associated at the conclusion of the poem with the Christ and the attending angels, the temptations can be reconciled with the divine nature of Christ; but they must be reconciled only in a manner that Christ, or God alone, can determine. Human beings must accept this distinction on faith. That such an acceptance conflicts with our rational and mundane knowledge and desires is inevitable, as is the pain that we experience. But the pain itself is part of our ultimate redemption. The triumphant joy in the divine meaning of Christ's sojourn on earth and the painful sorrow of the human response to this sojourn are brought together even more clearly in the final lines of this poem. We see here the contrast between Christ among the angels and Christ in "his mother's house."

The "angelic quires" (IV. 596–635) recall the story of Christ's beginnings as the "True image of the Father," through Satan's fall from heaven, and the final conquest over Satan by Christ's ability to resist temptation. Nothing, it should be noted, is said about the Passion. For in the angelic sense Christ's mission on earth is a triumphant success, another manifestation of God's greatness and infinite love for man. The speech, or song, concludes with the command to Christ to rid the world of Satan:

Hail, Son of the Most High, heir of both worlds,
Queller of Satan, on thy glorious work
Now enter, and begin to save mankind. (IV. 633–35)

The angels bring Christ "on his way with joy," but Christ the man follows a different path. We see him now as a human being, no longer in the ambrosial valley eating fruits from the "Tree of Life." Instead, "he unobserved/Home to his mother's house private returned."

Douglas Bush has noted in his text the contrast here "between Christ's divinity and his humanity," and A. S. P. Woodhouse has shown how this reference to Mary's house turns our thoughts back to Book I, in which Mary recounts her premonition that her great future, paradoxically, is her "exaltation to affliction high." We are at the end of the poem more aware than before as to how "high" this affliction will be. We have just read the lines in which Christ is accompanied by an angelic choir. But the "affliction" also bears a meaning to us that is closer to Mary than to the angels. For we have seen that the path of Christ leads not only to the crucifixion at the end, but to a path that involves even here on this earth, a dying to life.

It is a "dying" that we are told will lead to greater life for all men. And our faith in what we are told may erase the knowledge that is given to us by the sensible world. What we feel on our pulses as we see Christ dying to this world may indeed give way to a divine knowledge that tells us that Christ's pain is really bliss and that his affliction is really an exaltation.

But for faith to bring such untroubled acceptance in us, we would have to be saints; and most readers, I would assume, are not saints. The readers I am referring to would include Milton's comtemporaries as well as ours. The narrator of this poem, as Mrs. Lewalski has noted, is not a man who has fallen but should be thought of "as a man restored and redeemed by Christ's heroic action."[16] And for such a man, the pain of Christ's rejection of the world, including his rejection of life itself as we know it, may be accepted with triumphant song. The ordinary reader, however, is a fallen man. He may hope to be restored and redeemed at the second coming; but meanwhile he is prone to all of the human weaknesses, including a desire to enjoy whatever power he may in this sinful world. Such a man cannot share the responses of the narrator.

But such readers, and I include myself among them, can appreciate both the exaltation and the affliction that are present throughout the poem. Christ's rejection of Satan and of the world that Satan represents is a rejection of us. We understand and accept its necessity; but we also react as human beings to the terrible price that must be paid for our salvation. And this contrast between our understanding and our grief, a contrast implicit in the Passion, pervades the entire debate between the two protagonists. There is no need for the reader to reconcile these opposing feelings, since it is this opposition between the divine understanding and human grief that is the source of the tension that gives *Paradise Regained* its distinctive power.

NOTES

1. Arnold Stein, *Heroic Knowledge* (Minneapolis, Minn., 1957), p. 4.
2. W. W. Robson, "The Better Fortitude," in *The Living Milton*, ed. Frank Kermode (London, 1960), p. 135.
3. Perhaps the earliest work in this enterprise is Merritt Y. Hughes' "The

Christ of *Paradise Regained* and the Renaissance Heroic Tradition," *SP*
XXV (1938), 254–71. The most recent is Barbara Lewalski's *Milton's
Brief Epic* (Providence, R.I., 1966).

4. Robson, op. cit., p. 131.

5. Stein, op. cit., p. 131.

6. Northrop Frye, *The Return of Eden* (Toronto, 1965), p. 134.

7. In his *De Doctrina Christiana,* Milton affirms the dual nature of Christ
as both God and man. For a recent commentary, see J. Max Patrick, *The
Prose of John Milton* (Garden City, N.Y., 1967), pp. 647–48.

8. Frye, op. cit., pp. 122–23.

9. A. S. P. Woodhouse, "The Theme and Pattern of *Paradise Regained,"*
UTQ XXV (1955–56), 167.

10. Ibid. p. 168.

11. Frye, op. cit., p. 123.

12. E. M. W. Tillyard, *Studies in Milton* (London, 1951), p. 306.

13. Stein, op. cit., p. 101. Barbara Lewalski makes a similar distinction
between *scientia* and *sapientia* in *Milton's Brief Epic* (Providence, R.I.,
1966), p. 290.

14. Barbara Lewalski, *Milton's Brief Epic* (Providence, R.I., 1966), p. 310.

15. Ibid., p. 313.

16. Ibid., p. 327.

VII

The Unwilling Martyrdom
in *Samson Agonistes*

As MANY READERS have noticed, Milton's Samson is in many ways a counterpart to his Christ in *Paradise Regained*. But unlike the Christ who turns away gladly from this world to embrace a martyrdom, Samson is very much part of this world. The military victories that Christ disdained Samson seeks, and to Samson God's greatness can be shown only in the tangible, visible victories that all men can enjoy. The reader in this poem has no difficulty in identifying himself with the hero. If Samson's final action transforms him into a martyr, he is an unwilling martyr, as I intend to show here. And in doing so, I will try to refute a prevalent belief among present Miltonists that Samson is a Christian hero who triumphs over his despair by accepting God's actions, even when these actions result in blindness and captivity.

According to one critic, "it is this moral triumph, the survival of faith, which is the true subject of *Samson*."[1] And another critic finds that by combining his ability as a warrior with the fortitude of a Christian, Samson gains not only "the crown of martyrdom but also the public approbation of a conquering hero."[2] There is, it must be granted, strong evidence for interpreting the play as the triumph of a Christian hero, as we shall see when we come to a discussion of the Chorus. But the reconciliation that is arrived at intellectually by the Chorus, and also by Manoa, does not take into account the grief and the despair that permeates this entire work. As we have tried to show in the previous chapters, the imaginative experience of any great work goes far beyond the official or ostensible morality that is

93

embodied in it. *Samson Agonistes* is no exception. The response of many readers to the pain and humiliation of the hero, even at the moment of his triumph, makes it necessary to look for something more in this poem than the portrait of a Christian hero.

One such response by a critic who is sensitive to the emotions that *Samson* actually produces on most readers is particularly significant: We receive from this play, Isabel MacCaffrey concludes, an "impression of claustrophobia, of blind, fettered power and controlled ferocity," as well as "the sense of unbearable frustration and tension."[3] We can account for such a feeling in many ways; but, I believe, we can do so best by going beyond the didactic interpretations that are so prevalent among those Milton scholars who are determined to find in Samson the qualities of a Christian martyr. For, as we have tried to show in the preceding chapters, the greatness of a poem does not depend on the greatness of the hero or the nobility of the feelings that the poet takes as his subject. As critics we should be chiefly concerned with what the poet makes out of his ideas and beliefs. Even more sharply than in *Paradise Lost*, the imaginative experience of *Samson Agonistes* is based not only on Milton's faith but also on his doubt in God's justice. Samson's blindness, I intend to show here, is not only physical but also a sign of his inability to see the justice of God. Of course, like Milton himself, Samson wants desperately to *see* this justice. He wants above all to have his faith in God restored. And it is this conflict between what he wants to see and what he in fact does see (or fails to see) that provides the emotional and thematic center of the poem. It is the unresolved conflict, not the return of Samson to complete faith that lies at the core of his tragic experience.

It should no longer be necessary to defend an interpretation which may go beyond the expressed statements made in the poem, or beyond the ideas that were held by 17th-century readers. But even those readers who prefer to see a literary work tied down quite firmly to its author and to its historical period can hardly maintain that the author of *Paradise Lost* was incapable of some ambivalence towards the justice of God's ways. Nor would it be difficult to develop the oft-noted resemblance between Samson's position and that of Milton himself, the "great deliverer now . . . Blind among enemies," in order to find justification for Samson's questioning of God's ways to "his faithful champion." But the biographical interpretation of this poem has been done extremely well by others, particularly James Holly Hanford, whose work will be referred to later. This essay will concern itself only with the action and imagery of the poem in an effort to account for its distinctive power.

Douglas Bush, in his edition of the poems, has suggested that Samson is asking for more than the help of a fellow prisoner, in the opening lines of the poem: "A little onward lend thy guiding hand./To these dark steps, a little further on." Samson is, unconsciously of course, asking for God's help, as well as for the help of a fellow slave. But if the "guiding hand" has a spiritual meaning, so can the "dark steps," and even more, the blindness that causes these steps to be dark. The image of light, with its variants such as "sun," "dayspring" and "sight" have a traditional association with wisdom and truth. And in Milton's poetry this significance is stronger than in that of almost any other poet. Darkness also has its traditional as well as its specifically Miltonic significance of ignorance. In this context, however, Samson is denied sight and light not only as a. punishment for his sin, but as a symbol of his inability to understand, to "see," why God has brought about such terrible suffering to His champion.

> Why was my breeding ordered and prescribed
> As of a person separate to God,
> Designed for great exploits, if I must die
> Betrayed, captíved, and both my eyes put out. . . . (30–33)

Of course Samson accepts his punishment; he is by no means a 20th-century atheist or existentialist. But it is also true that he cannot understand the logic of a Divine Providence which places this greater deliverer "Eyeless in Gaza at the mill with slaves." Much as he wants to understand or *see* God's actions as justifiable in human terms, Samson is unable to repress his natural bitterness and helplessness at what seems like a "blind Fury." What we have in the opening scene, therefore, is a conflict between a strong desire to accept without question and an even stronger impulse to "quarrel with the will" of God. Samson means just what he says when he proclaims:

> But peace! I must not quarrel with the will
> Of highest dispensation, which herein
> Haply had ends above my reach to know. . . . (60–63)

The significant point, however, and one that is often missed by the critics, is that Samson does not do what he wants, but what he cannot help doing, that is, to cry aloud in agony at the impenetrability of God's ways:

> O dark, dark, dark, amid the blaze of noon,
> Irrecoverably dark, total eclipse
> Without all hope of day!
> O first-created beam, and thou great Word,
> "Let there be light, and light was over all";
> Why am I thus bereaved thy prime decree?
> The Sun to me is dark
> And silent as the Moon,
> When she deserts the night,
> Hid in her vacant interlunar Cave. (80–89)

It is not merely the sun that is dark, but in a sense God's ways also in that (like the moon) He is "silent" and does not reveal to Samson the reason for the chain of events that has brought about this terrible calamity.

This last statement requires some further explanation, since many critics have assumed that it is not God but Samson who is responsible for the terrible events that have just taken place. As Samson himself asserts,

> Yet stay, let me not rashly call in doubt
> Divine prediction; what if all foretold
> Had been fulfilled but through mine own default?
> Whom have I to complain of but myself? (43–46)

But as Milton of all men would most readily realize, God's ways are not so easily seen, particularly to one who does not have a "celestial Light" to "Shine inward." If it is true that God brought about Samson's decision to marry Dalila, then was it not God also who gave him that particular weakness that prompted Samson to reveal the secret of his strength? For some critics the answer to such questions leads into theology and logic, and to subsequent arguments among Catholics, Calvinists, Arminians and agnostics. What is essential, however, for those who are concerned with the poem as an imaginative experience, is that (rightly or wrongly) Samson does in fact feel that God is responsible for his pain. This feeling does not lead him to excuse his own actions, nor does it even allow him, at least consciously, to lose his trust in the rightness of God's dispensation. But simply as a suffering human being (not as a Christian, Stoic or agnostic) Samson expresses, in the most powerful lines of his soliloquy, his grief at not being able to *see* why God has placed him in this darkness "Without all hope of day!" The physical blindness can of course *symbolize* Samson's inability to understand God's ways. But it is better, as recent students of Milton's language have made us aware, to think of the image as *simultaneously* physical and spiritual (Isabel MacCaffrey, *"Paradise Lost" as Myth*). The light which "so necessary is to life/And almost life itself" is both physical sight and "That light [which] is in the soul." The indivisibility of these two meanings is further emphasized by the juxtaposition of the "Word" which created light and the light itself: "O first-created beam, and thou great Word/'Let there be light and light was over all.' "

There are of course a number of answers to Samson's question, and Milton wants us to feel, even if like Samson we do not *see,* the presence of a force that transcends our doubts. Samson may not be able to see "the light;" but just as he can feel the sun or the "blaze of noon" while blind, so he can also feel or believe in his soul that there is some rational answer for his suffering—if he could only *see* it. His despair is therefore brought about not by unbelief but by faith, a faith, however, that cannot be satisfied by his reason.

This same conflict between the justice which Samson wants to see and the darkness, in both senses of the word, which surrounds him, can also be found in the speeches of the Chorus which close this scene. Here again we have the admonition to "Tax not divine disposal" (210) while at the same time the

Chorus continually wonders at and questions this same "divine disposal." "Just are the ways of God, and justifiable to men," is the ostensible theme of the speech; but "justifiable" we soon learn refers only to the realm of possibility. There is no actual justification, no answer to those who "doubt his ways not just,/As to his own edicts found contradicting." There is undoubtedly a strong desire that the justice of God be made manifest to us; but in the actual experience of the present, there is no "self-satisfying solution." No more than Samson is the Chorus able to circumscribe its "wandering thoughts." The very warning against being involved in "perplexities" is followed by an attempted explanation as to why God told Samson "To seek in marriage that fallacious bride,/Unclean, unchaste." And the final lines of the argument counter the impulses to deny Reason (which is expressed in the first line) with the equally strong lines affirming the human need to find reasons:

> Down, Reason, then, at least vain reasonings down,
> Though Reason here aver
> That moral verdict quits her of unclean:
> Unchaste was subsequent; her stain, not his. (322–25)

That the reasoning is "vain" in God's eyes does not negate the human need to rely on reason, to seek some explanation for the fact that "this great deliverer" is now "Eyeless in Gaza at the mill with slaves." The urgent need to see the light, in both senses of the word, and the equally strong sense that there is no hope for a recovery of that light are at the center of the conflict that rages within Samson.

This conflict pervades the entire play, and is even present, in a somewhat different key, in Manoa's speech which opens the second scene. After recounting once again the contrast between the great expectations which God allowed Manoa to have for his son and the terrible sufferings that resulted, Manoa tries to find some explanation in a hope that God will not "overwhelm" with "foul indignities" those who were "chosen once/To worthiest deeds." But it is obvious that, at least for the present, God has done just that. Samson offers a better explanation for what are, obviously, "foul indignities," by reiterating that he himself "has brought them on." But the actual recital of his experience with his two Philistine brides makes clear that if Samson did indeed bring on these evils, it was only because some greater power seemed bent on overcoming his natural resistance. The very movement of the lines, the sense running beyond the meter yet never obscuring the action, makes us feel the irresistible force of the temptation offered by Dalila:

> Yet the fourth time, when must'ring all her wiles,
> With blandished parleys, feminine assaults,
> Tongue-batteries, she surceased not day or night
> To storm me over-watched, and wearied out,
> At times when men seek most repose and rest,
> I yielded, and unlocked her all my heart. . . . (402–407)

It is hard to believe, after such a description, that only "a grain of manhood, well resolved [could] . . . easily have shook off all her snares." And Samson's next speech indicates that it is God, not Samson, who must act to set things right again. There is no logical necessity for assuming that the person or force who is able to set things right is the cause of the evil, and Samson does not make this implication. What he does recognize, however, is that, rightly or wrongly, the recent events have "oped the mouths/Of idolists and atheists; have brought scandal to Israel." For these events are undoubtedly caused by power far greater than that of any individual action. Samson's reference to the "atheists" is also significant in that they reflect doubts that he himself feels. Samson is not one of these atheists; if he were he would not be so pained. But "this doubt in feeble hearts," even if the hearts belong to others, is his "chief affliction, shame and sorrow,/The anguish of my soul."

To follow Samson's feelings at this point, we must push aside any particular view as to what kind of man he is supposed to be, or, what is often the same thing, what kind of man the critic would like him to be. It is not a religious or a philosophic context, but the context of this particular poem that should be primary. And in this context the anguish, affliction, shame, and sorrow are not to be praised or blamed, but to be seen as the inevitable counterparts of his physical blindness. While the

"mouths" of atheists are open, Samson's eyes are closed. The
"blind mouths" of *Lycidas* might seem here to underline the
paradox. And the only solution is for God to reverse this situation by some drastic action that will silence the mouths of
atheists and open the eyes of the believers. As so often in Milton,
despair about the present is balanced by hope for the future:
"He, be sure/*Will* not connive or linger . . . But will arise and
his great name assert." The italics are not Milton's, but the
reliance on future events is. As the next speech of Samson's
makes clear, he is less concerned with the pain of his physical
punishment than with the "anguish" brought about by the
doubt as to God's ways. Calling for a victory of God over Dagon
is not a metaphor for a victory of the Hebrews over the Philistines, but a literal statement. For it is God who has to be
justified, not the mortals. The trial that so many of the critics
mention concerns God more than Samson. It is God who must
perform some action that will allow Samson to see the light of
truth, even if the light of the sun will forever be denied to him.

Such a view of the play can also help us to understand Samson's unwillingness to be ransomed, pardoned, or comforted in
any way. "To what end should I seek it?" he asks even in regard
to life itself. The answer of Manoa, that it is wrong to
choose death to avoid pain and disgrace, only deals with the
outward aspect of Samson's condition. There is no answer to the
inward anguish. Why should His most devoted servant
"whose birth was from Heaven foretold" end up "despoiled/
Shaven, and disarmed among . . . enemies"? Samson is quite
willing to take the blame and beg "His pardon." But if God
is, for any reason, willing to allow His chosen servant "to sit
idle on the household hearth/A burdensome drone" (566–67),
then Samson can see no alternative but to call on death to
"Hasten the welcome end of all my pain."

Manoa continues to urge his son to hold on to life, even if he
must remain at home "unemployed, with age outworn." For
perhaps in the future God will perform a miracle and give
Samson his sight again: "Cause light within thy eyes to
spring,/Wherewith to serve him better than thou hast."
(584–85) Such a reply does not of course answer Samson's
fundamental question, the question of why God has so far acted

with such cruelty to one who was previously so favored. And why should Samson hope for a miracle from a God who has taken away from him even his natural powers?

> All otherwise my thoughts portend,
> That these dark orbs no more shall treat with light,
> Nor th' other light of life continue long,
> But yield to double darkness nigh at hand. . . . (590–93)

The double meaning of light is again relevant here. The "other light" is of course life itself. But the continual emphasis on light and darkness does suggest that Samson's blindness is again, as in the earlier scene, a symbol of his inability to see what he wants to see more than anything else—the justice of God's actions. And that he is convinced that he can never again see his God as Divine Providence rather than as blind Fate is made clear in the long soliloquy that begins with the lament that the torments which he suffers are not confined.

> To the body's wounds and sores,
> . . . .
> But must secret passage find
> To th'inmost mind. . . . (607, 610–11)

And Samson goes on to compare his thoughts with "wounds immedicable" which "Rankle and fester, and gangrene,/To black mortification." What these thoughts are is made clear in the concluding paragraph:

> I was his nursling once and choice delight,
> His destined from the womb,
> Promised by heavenly message twice descending.
> Under his special eye
> Abstemious I grew up and thrived amain;
> He led me on to mightiest deeds
> Above the nerve of mortal arm
> Against the uncircumcised, our enemies.
> But now hath cast me off as never known,
> And to those cruel enemies,
> Whom I by his appointment had provoked,

Left me all helpless with th'irreparable loss
Of sight, reserved alive to be repeated
The subject of their cruelty or scorn. (633–46)

Although this passage is reminiscent of Adam's complaint
against God in Book X of *Paradise Lost,* Samson does not even
try to find a reason for God's seemingly arbitrary actions. Completely overcome with a darkness so deep and powerful that
it must denote more than physical deprivation, Samson asks
only for death, the "double darkness" that he referred to in his
reply to his father:

Nor am I in the list of them that hope;
Hopeless are all my evils, all remédiless;
This one prayer yet remains, might I be heard,
No long petition—speedy death,
The close of all my miseries, and the balm. (647–51)

At this the Chorus delivers its longest and most famous
speech, which gives greater amplitude, if not depth, to the
anguish of Samson. The Stoic's answer to human suffering,
which extolls "patience as the truest fortitude," is dismissed. For

with th'afflicted in his pangs their sound
Little prevails, or rather seems a tune
Harsh, and of dissonant mood from his complaint. (660–62)

And the Chorus then goes on to what is perhaps Milton's ultimate expression of his doubt concerning the justice, if not the
very presence, of God.

God of our Fathers, what is man!
That thou towards him with hand so various
Or might I say contrarious
.Temper'st thy providence through his short course,
Not evenly,
· ·
Nor only dost degrade them, or remit
To life obscur'd, which were a fair dismission,
But throws't them lower than thou didst exalt them high,
· ·

Just or unjust, alike seem miserable,
For oft alike, both come to evil end.

                                        (667–71, 687–89, 703–04)

Stanley Fish's recent comment is appropriate here: "This is
not a Hebrew complaint (except as it echoes Job whose own
credentials as a pious Jew have been challenged) but a *human*
complaint, occasioned by the willing suffering of a fellow creature and uttered apart from any prior theorizing on the relationship between God and man."[4]

Only one who can go beyond the natural world, who can "feel
within/Some source of consolation from above" can hope to
avoid the complete prostration of Samson. But nothing that is
said in the rest of the speech gives any possibility of "consolation
from above." The complaint that God punishes most severe-
ly those whom He has singled out for greatness applies not only
to Samson, but more specifically as many commentators have
pointed out, to Milton himself and to the events of the Restora-
tion. But these personal references do not remove us from Samson's plight; they only give greater emphasis to those feelings in
the poem which are in continual opposition to our faith in
God's providence. There remains, as J. H. Hanford remarked
many years ago, "an irreducible element in the midst of Milton's faith—a sense as keen as Shakespeare's of the reality of
suffering which neither the assurance of God's special favors to
himself nor his resolute insistence on the final triumph of his
righteousness can blot out."[5]

That God's providence will, however, be finally reasserted is
still present in our minds. But at this point it is felt more as a
hope and as a need than as a reality. What we see even as we
move on to the entrance of Dalila is not the intervention of God
but the development of another aspect of Samson: his need
for action. Thus far Samson has had only a passive role; he has
had to exercise what the Chorus will later describe as "patience
. . . the exercise of saints." And as we have seen, this quality is
something that is alien to Samson, who can see in suffering not
the preparation of a more-than-human heroism but only the
cruelty of an inexplicable God. As a warrior, as a man of action,
as a human being, not a Christ, Samson can serve God only by

his "invincible might." This aspect of Samson will appear openly with the entrance of Harapha, but the origin of the active
impulse, and therefore the turning point of the play, is present
in his encounter with Dalila. To refer again to Hanford's early
essay, "the intensity of Samson's pain lasts only so long as he
remains inactive. His lyric elaboration of his inward woe is
immediately followed by the unexpected visits of his foes."[6]

The effects of Dalila's visit have been described by many
critics, and there is little doubt that she is able to stir Samson
out of his torpor into anger and eventually into action. But
there is another aspect of this encounter that goes below the
surface of the scene and brings us back to Samson's quarrel with
God. Dalila reminds us of Samson's earlier suffering as well as
prepares us for his future encounter with Harapha. In the first
speech Dalila announces her intention "To lighten what thou
sufferest, and appease/Thy mind with what amends is in my
power" (744–45). Of course, "lighten" means relieve, but it can
also remind us of the earlier connotations of light, insofar as
her words are intended to "appease" Samson's mind. The intention is not realized. Ingenious as this "sorceress" may be, Samson is able to see nothing in her arguments, although he is
stirred for a brief moment by memories of their former intimacy. But the memories serve only to increase his anger at her
betrayal:

> I before all the daughters of my Tribe
> And of my nation chose thee from among
> My enemies, loved thee, as too well thou know'st
> Too well; unbosomed all my secrets to thee,
> Not out of levity, but overpow'red
> By thy request, who could deny thee nothing;
> Yet now am judged an enemy. (876–82)

Like the actions of God, the actions of Dalila are incredible to
Samson. How could she to whom he "unbosomed all [his]
secrets," and who it seemed from all appearances loved and
admired him, become an accomplice to such a cruel act?
Nothing that Dalila can say, and her excuses are extremely
ingenious, can make any impression on Samson:

Thy fair enchanted cup and warbling charms
No more on me have power, their force is nulled;
So much of adder's wisdom have I learnt
To fence my ear against thy sorceries. (934–37)

Of course Dalila is not God, and God's justification for His
actions are not "sorceries." But the sense of betrayal is remarkably similar. How could God have allowed His great champion
to suffer so pitiably, Samson had cried out earlier in the play,
and his cry had been echoed by the Chorus. And now Samson is
confounded by the undeniable but also incredible fact that he
was betrayed by his own wife:

in my flower of youth and strength when all men
Loved, honored, feared me, thou alone could hate me,
Thy husband, slight me, sell me, and forego me. . . . (937–40)

In neither case does Samson ever forget his own responsibility for his plight. At no time in his quarrel with God did he ever
fail to admit his own guilt. And to Dalila's argument that she
was led to her betrayal by his example, Samson is quite willing
to agree:

I gave, thou say'st, the example,
I led the way—bitter reproach, but true;
I to myself was false ere thou to me. . . . (822–24)

But *his* weakness does not excuse *hers;* he gives her the same
forgiveness that he gives himself—none. "Such pardon therefore
as I give my wicked folly/Take to thy wicked deed." The
parallel between Samson's attitude toward Dalila in this scene
and his attitude in the earlier scenes is thus intensified. Samson
never tries to hide his own sense of guilt and his own responsibility for his defeat. But at the same time, he cannot
understand why a merciful God who seemed to favor him, and a
beautiful wife who seemed to love and admire him, should
allow him to suffer such pain.

What Samson cannot say to God directly, he can without
compunction say to another human being. In thus breaking out
into bitter hatred towards Dalila, and in reassuring himself that

he was an innocent victim of arts too devious for him to untangle, Samson is also giving vent to those very human feelings of anger, hatred, and self-justification which he had to repress when he addressed God. The scene with Dalila thus furthers the action of the play, not by allowing Samson to show his wisdom or his faith (anyone in his position would resist Dalila), but by allowing him to express his pent-up anger and his self-justification without any hint of blasphemy. Samson may seem less like a classical hero or a Christian martyr with such an interpretation, but he is also a much more consistent and credible human being.

Even more then in the meeting with Dalila, it is hard to explain the encounter with Harapha if we confine ourselves to either a literal or a religious interpretation of Samson's actions. It is almost puerile in a drama of such seriousness to have a major scene revolve around the curiosity of some braggart concerning the stoutness of Samson's limbs. Yet it is difficult, despite the ingenuity of many critics, to see a great spiritual recovery in Samson's boasting of his former deeds or in his threat to break Harapha's head "with an oaken staff." If we look at this scene as a development of the main theme, however, the physical strength can be seen as a manifestation of God's power—that power which was quiescent in the early scenes, which came to the surface for a moment in the threat to tear Dalila "joint by joint," and which will shortly be turned against both the Philistines and Samson himself. That this power belongs more to God than to Samson, and that it is God who is on trial rather than Samson, is made explicit in this scene.

The scene opens, it is true, with a purely personal encounter between the two giants. But since Harapha comes only "each limb to survey," there is hardly any development. The scene gains momentum only when Samson describes the conflict as one between Dagon and God. At this point Harapha returns us to the central conflict by making explicit what was only implied in the earlier scenes, namely, that recent events should remove any faith in the justice and power of Samson's God.

> Presume not on thy God, whate'er he be;
> Thee he regards not, owns not, hath cut off

Quite from his people, and delivered up
Into thy enemies' hand, permitted them
To put out both thine eyes, and fettered send thee
Into the common prison. . . . (1156–61)

Samson cannot dispute the facts; and even the conclusion drawn
from these facts, that God has no regard for his faithful champion, is not very different from Samson's earlier feelings. What
Samson does, therefore, is to give two answers. First, he shifts
the blame to himself: "these evils I deserve and more." But, as
if realizing that the shift of blame does not really answer the
charge that God has forsaken him, Samson quickly offers a
second answer: a challenge directed at Harapha "to the trial of
mortal fight/By combat to decide whose god is God." For it is
clear that in this particular context Harapha can be answered
only by a visible and concrete sign of God's favor.

It is not that Samson doesn't believe in his own responsibility
for his suffering. It is simply that he is a human being and not a
theologian; and as such he could understand God's beneficence
much better if he were enabled to tear Harapha limb from
limb. Samson cannot understand a kingdom that is not of this
world. In challenging Harapha to physical combat, Samson is
doing more than showing us his renewed strength. He is also
challenging God to give him a visible sign of His power. Samson's renewed strength is, of course, a sign of God's power. And
Samson's willingness to use his strength is, as Don Cameron
Allen has pointed out, a sign of his turning away from despair.[7]
But what most critics do not see is that when Harapha walks
away from Samson, we should recognize that God is refusing to
satisfy Samson's plea for the "invincible might" with which to
overcome the heathen and "By combat to decide whose god is
God" (1176). "Whate'er be," God is unwilling to prove his
divinity by such a test. Samson realizes this quite clearly, and
returns to his earlier mood of despair:

But come what will, my deadliest foe will prove
My speediest friend, by death to rid me hence,
The worst that he can give, to me the best. (1261–64)

The conflict between the kind of action that Samson wants

and the kind of action that God has evidently decreed for him is
made explicit by the Chorus in the lines immediately following:

> Oh how comely it is and how reviving
> To the Spirits of just men long opprest,
> When God into the hands of their deliverer
> Puts invincible might
> To quell the mighty of the earth, th' oppressor,
> The brute and boist'rous force of violent men,
> Hardy and industrious to support
> Tyrannic power, but raging to pursue
> The righteous and all such as honour truth!
> He all their ammunition
> And feats of war defeats
> With plain heroic magnitude of mind
> And celestial vigour arm'd;
> Their armories and magazines contemns,
> Renders them useless, while
> With winged expedition
> Swift as the lightning glance he executes
> His errand on the wicked, who surprised
> Lose their defence, distracted and amazed.
>   But patience is more oft the exercise
> Of saints, the trial of their fortitude,
> Making them each his own deliverer,
> And victor over all
> That tyranny or fortune can inflict,
> Either of these is in thy lot,
> Samson, with might endu'd
> Above the sons of men; but sight bereaved
> May chance to number thee with those
> Whom patience finally must crown. (1268–96)

Both forms of action are equally valuable to God, or at least
they would seem so to Milton. And we know that by his concluding action Samson will overcome in a physical sense "the
brute and boisterous force of violent men." But all that he
knows at this moment is that he must allow his trial to be not of
brute strength but of his "fortitude." And it is precisely this

quality, this Christlike separation from violent action, that Samson cannot fully appreciate. It is not easy for anyone to accept suffering so as to become a "victor over all/That tyranny or fortune can inflict." It is particularly difficult for a warrior whose strength had clearly been a gift of God, "Designed for great exploits. . . ." (32) Samson's disappointment at not being allowed to exercise his strength is, therefore, a reflection of his deeper disappointment at not being able to understand the ways of God. Samson is quite conscious of the sinfulness of this feeling. He knows that even if the one talent lodged in him is useless, he must still serve God. But it goes against the very core of his being to stand and wait. Such a sharp conflict between his active impulses and the passivity which it seems that God has decreed for him helps to explain the ambiguous action in the next scene.

Unable to use his strength *against* the enemy, Samson is naturally bitter at being asked to use it for their amusement. It also seems likely, in view of what has occurred until now, that God has no need for this particular man's work, and that Samson would serve Him best by merely bearing his yoke. But Samson's returning strength, his "rousing motions," reveals to us his unconquerable desire for action. Without in any way denying the reasons which Samson gives for his changed decision—prudence and the sense of a divine mission—we should also see his willingness to attend the Philistine games as an expression of the deepest impulse of his character.

Even when Samson is first led into the theater, "In their stately livery clad . . .," we get a sense of his finally being in his element. The tricks he performs are, of course, for the amusement of his enemies. And the shouts of the people are in praise of "their god . . ./Who had made their dreadful enemy their thrall" (1621–22). But the "incredible, stupendous force" with which he performs the tasks belongs only to Samson. The strength that was chained when he confronted Harapha is now being released, and in a few moments this strength will be released against the enemy. As Samson raises his mighty arms to pull down the pillars, he is once again the military hero chosen by God to destroy "th'oppressor,/The brute and boist'rous force of violent men."

The irony of the final scene, that in destroying the Philistines he destroys himself, underlines the irony of his entire life. Once again his strength is self-defeating. We are made to see (by the words of the Messenger) a giant lifting his powerful arms to grasp the pillars and shake the roof. But as our eyes move up to the highest point, the downward motion follows immediately. The roof comes down, burying Samson along with the proud and joyous Philistines beneath the ruins of the temple. The whole picture impresses us with the self-defeating nature, the futility, of action. The action destroys alike "just or unjust," and gives to Samson's strength that ambivalent edge which turns his salvation into his death.

Just how closely allied are the truimph and the defeat can also be seen in the images used by the Messenger in his report of the action in the temple. Such words as "flame," "dragon," and "eagle" indicate forces that are in themselves directionless and amoral; they destroy just or unjust alike. The blindness that was the dominant image in the earlier part of the play is again of significance here:

> But he, though blind of sight,
> Despised and thought extinguished quite,
> With inward eye illuminated
> His fiery virtue roused
> From under ashes into sudden flame. . . . (1687–91)

To Isabel MacCaffrey, these final images succeed in inverting the initial situation. "At the beginning Samson is 'dark in light exposed'; at the end 'his fiery virtue,' a light hidden in darkness, breaks out 'from under ashes into sudden flame.' The images thus epitomize the dramatic action, which turns on a peripety or reversal as Aristotle prescribed."[8] One might add that the fire and flame also represent the energy that has until now been quiescent in Samson, and is now being released to destroy not only his enemies but Samson himself. But the real irony, one that is central to the main action of the play, remains in the contrast between blindness and sight. There is no doubt that Samson's "inward eye" is now "illuminated." But what does he see?

Not, I believe, what he had hoped to see throughout the play: a clear explanation of why God had caused His champion to suffer. For, as we have tried to show, the justice of God's actions is symbolized by light, a light which Samson cannot see, physically or spiritually. And since Samson remains blind physically, even as he regains his strength in the final scene, there is no metaphorical reason for believing that he has regained his faith in God's justice. What he can see with his "inward eye," what is actually "illuminated" can be determined only by the reader who takes into account everything that occurs.

And for many such readers, there is no complete reversal at the end. Despite the statement of Manoa, "Nothing is here for tears, nothing to wail" (1721), and despite the conclusion of the Chorus that

> All is best, though we oft doubt,
> What the unsearchable dispose
> Of highest wisdom brings about. . . . (1745–47)

we feel that what Samson sees and feels as he pulls down the pillars must include the pain that he has felt all along, as well as the joy at the release of his heroic energy. Some readers want to push aside Manoa's sentiments as coming from an impercipient person who never gets below the surface of his son's agony. But the Chorus expresses essentially the same attitude. Nor is there anything in the play to indicate that these passages, expressing the fierce joy of victory and the complete acceptance of God's ways, should be interpreted as ironic. Arnold Stein offers us another way of looking at these passages by suggesting that the Chorus (and Semichorus) are part of "a ritual demanded by Decorum. The return of Samson to his God is a return to his people, and they must, since the tragedy is a shared experience, not walk away numb and dumb. They need this expression of human decency and dignity, to mark the return of Samson to them and to mark their return, through shared experience, closer to God whose 'faithful Champion' Samson has 'in the close' proved to be."[9]

The idea of a "need" on the part of the spectators, both

within the play and outside of the play, is particularly helpful at this point. For the ideas and feelings in these speeches of Manoa and the Chorus are precisely those that we ought to have, or "need," to express our closeness to both the hero and to God. But these public or official feelings may very well differ from those that we have as private persons affected by grief, despair, and dumb amazement at the inexplicable ways of God. There is nothing hypocritical or mysterious about any group of people using language, not as an expression of spontaneous feeling, but as an expression of feelings which we do not so much possess as desire, or as Mr. Stein puts it, "need." The consolatory lines in the conclusion, therefore, are to be accepted only as it concerns what we are *supposed* to learn from the events of the play. They do not mark a reversal, an Aristotelian peripety, since they do not allow Samson or the readers to really "see" the justice of God's ways, or at least, if we do, it is not the kind of justice that Samson had hoped for. Nor does an affirmation of God's presence and even of His justice necessarily remove the anguish experienced as the result of a justice that we ourselves cannot feel, as the "terrible sonnets" of Hopkins make clear.

The final action of Samson is the culmination of his struggle, suppressed but by no means extinguished throughout the play, to act in human terms, rather than to suffer patiently as one of God's saints. That his action, when it does come about, turns upon itself, that the heroic act results in the death of the hero, is an inevitable irony. And it may even reveal, as William Madsen has pointed out, that military action "is inferior to the patience exercised by the saints."[10] But what is clear to God (or to the theologian who interprets God's will) is not necessarily what we see as mortal men. And Samson, completely human, strives for a victory in this world, a victory that he could *see*. He is not at all like the Christ whom we have seen in *Paradise Regained*, the Christ who seeks a victory that cannot be found in this world. Samson is quite human; if he is a type of Christ, he is, as Mr. Madsen suggests, an antitype; "we must insist that his significance for the Christian reader lies primarily in his inability to measure up to the heroic norm delineated in *Paradise Regained*."[11]

This contrast between Samson and Christ is a welcome correc-
tive to the efforts of those scholars who are so preoccupied with
what Samson ought to be (according to some medieval tradition) that they overlook what he actually does in this particular
poem. But Mr. Madsen has a mistaken view of what literature
should do when he *judges* Samson according to some heroic
norm. Not only is Samson unlike Christ, as Madsen correctly
reveals, but Samson is not supposed to be Christ. We are, or
should be, trying to understand particular poems, not judging
characters according to some moral scale. We will get closer, I
believe, to the distinctive power of *Samson Agonistes* if we
forget about an heroic norm, in a classical, a Christian, or an
existentialist sense, and see Samson as a human being who, like
his creator, could never reconcile the world that he desired with
the world that he had to accept. Only in this way can we
respond fully to the "impression of claustrophobia, of blind,
fettered power and controlled ferocity," as well as to "the sense of
unbearable frustration and tension" which Mrs. MacCaffrey
finds evident in the very texture of the play. The greatness of
Samson Agonistes does not depend on the reconciliation of the
hero or of the audience to the ways of God, but on its power to
bring to the highest pitch the contradiction between human
desires and divine purpose.

NOTES

1. *Samson Agonistes,* ed. F. T. Prince (London, 1957), p. 13.
2. A. B. Chambers, "Wisdom and Fortitude in *Samson Agonistes,*" *PMLA*
LXXVIII (1963), p. 320. More recently Anthony Low has written a convincing refutation of those who see Samson as an entirely passive martyr by
showing that Samson's martial activity is just as strong as his patience:
"Action and Suffering: *Samson Agonistes* and the Irony of Alternatives,"
PMLA 84 (1969), 514–19. But Mr. Low continues to see in Samson's action
a manifestation of God's justice and mercy.
3. Isabel MacCaffrey, *Samson Agonistes and the Shorter Poems of Milton*
(New York, 1967), p. xxxvi.
4. Stanley Fish, "Question and Answer in *Samson Agonistes,*" *The Critical Quarterly* (Autumn 1969), p. 247.
5. J. H. Hanford, "*Samson Agonistes* and Milton in Old Age," in *John
Milton, Poet and Humanist* (Cleveland, 1966), p. 280. (The essay originally appeared in 1925.)
6. Ibid. p. 285.

7. D. H. Allen, *The Harmonious Vision* (Baltimore, 1954).
8. MacCaffrey, op. cit., pp. xxxii–xxxv.
9. Arnold Stein, *Heroic Knowledge* (Minneapolis, 1957), p. 182.
10. William Madsen, "From Shadowy Types to Truth," *The Lyric and Dramatic Milton*, ed. Joseph H. Summers (New York, 1965), p. 114.
11. Ibid., p. 114.

VIII

Concluding Notes

Milton's View of Poetry

ALL OF THE poems in this book have been discussed in somewhat different ways, and these differences reflect the fact that the relationship between the moral beliefs and the aesthetic significance varies from poem to poem. Nevertheless, at least two statements about this relationship can be applied to all of the poems: The moral beliefs, both explicit and implicit, are subjected to an experience within each poem which contradicts them in some essential way. But far from weakening these poems this contradiction between the beliefs and the poetic experience is the source of a tension that gives the poems their value for the modern reader. For example, in *Lycidas*, it is not the cogency of the doctrine of immortality but the conflict between that doctrine and the sense of loss felt by the poet that gives the poem its power. And we find *Paradise Lost* a moving poem not because of the poet's success in justifying God's ways to man, but because of the counterpoint between the need to find justice in His ways and the full portrayal of His arbitrary nature.

Objections to such interpretations are inevitable, and I have tried to meet some of them in the chapters on the individual poems. But there is another kind of objection, an objection not to the interpretation of any particular poem, but to the critical assumption that underlies my entire approach, that also deserves an answer. For, as I admitted in the first chapter, what is found valuable in any writer depends to some extent on the critic's basic assumptions about literature. And the assumption that is relevant here is that the greatness of a poem does not lie in its power to inculcate a moral feeling, but in its power to make the reader aware of a level of experience beyond the confines of our moral categories. The strength and the enduring qualities of Milton's poetry do not depend on its power to make us accept noble truths, but on its power to make us aware of the limitations of the moral categories when they are confronted by the complexities of human experience.

But even if we grant that readers in our own time respond to Milton's poetry for its literary rather than its moral significance, are we not violating Milton's intention? And even if a literary interpretation must disregard this intention, should we not at least admit that we are reading his poetry in a way that Milton himself would have opposed? I do not believe so. For although Milton's explicit statements about the function of poetry are moralistic, his actions would indicate that he was not so confident of the didactic power of poetry.

Few writers have been so strongly committed to moral action as John Milton. For more than twenty years he devoted himself to pamphleteering in the cause of what he considered religious, domestic, and political liberty. For ten years he was an important member of the Cromwell government, and was known throughout Europe as a defender of regicides. Even his devotion to poetry was, in his eyes, a means, no less effective than the pulpit, to inculcate moral virtue. Most students of Milton are familiar with his eloquent statements praising poetry for its moral value. Perhaps the most famous and most eloquent is in the autobiographical passage from *The Reason of Church Government Urged against Prelaty*, where Milton, after comparing a poet to a preacher, argues that the poet is even more powerful because he can teach "the whole book of sanctity and virtue . . . with such delight to those . . . who will not so much as look upon truth herself unless they see her elegantly dressed. . . ." And he urges the state to foster recitations of poetry as "graceful enticements to the love and practice of justice, temperance and fortitude, instructing and bettering the nation at all opportunities."

There is an irony in this statement that has not been noticed, and which exemplifies the distinction made in these essays, between Milton as poet and Milton as a prophet and revolutionary. For in the same paragraph in which he announces that poetry can be more effective than prose in inculcating moral virtue, Milton announces his decision to give up poetry so that he can play an effective role in the political and religious warfare of his time. In order to act effectively in behalf of his ideas, he will go against "the genial power of nature;" he will take up the use of his "left hand", and enter the political arena "in the cool element of prose."

No one would deny, of course, that arguments on church government or on divorce or on political liberty must be written in prose rather than in verse. But it is significant that with all of his confidence in the power of poetry to lead people to "justice, temperance and fortitude," Milton did not even attempt to write poetry (except for a few sonnets) during the years when he was engaged in the great political and religious crises. Despite the moral effects which he ascribes to literature, Milton seems to have felt that only prose (or prosaic sonnets) could reveal political truth or inspire his countrymen to fight for what he called Christian liberty. Only when he had given up all hope for a true reformation did he turn again to poetry.

These facts about Milton's life do not prove that he did not intend his final poems to have a moral effect. Nor would his intention be decisive in determining just how to interpret the poems. But that Milton himself, the great moralist among English poets, turned to prose whenever he felt the need for "instructing and bettering the nation," may very well be an indication that the mature Milton recognized that poetry had a different function, one quite separate from the "office of a pulpit."

But whatever may have been the case for Milton, and we can never determine his *intention*, the value of his poetry has far surpassed the value of his doctrines. Much as we may admire the man who entered into the political and religious controversies of his time, it is in his poetry that we can find that "new acquist/Of true experience" which goes beyond any doctrine and which cannot be separated from the literary experience itself.

Comus and the Sonnets

IN A BOOK on the major poems of Milton, the most conspicuous
omission is *Comus*. But it is generally agreed that the artistic
value of *Comus* is of a different kind than is found in the other
poems of Milton. There is wide disagreement on the meaning
of *Comus*.[1] But almost all critics agree on the fact that the
morality is definite. There is no ambivalence within the poem
about the value of Chastity. In rejecting the temptation of
Comus, the Lady is not made to sacrifice anything; she does not
lose one value in order to gain her good.

Cleanth Brooks and J. E. Hardy are among the few critics
who find a tension and dramatic irony in the action of this mask.
"The characters in *Comus* sometimes speak allegorically, in
their own right; but they are not themselves allegorical. The
pattern and significance in the action and imagery of the poem
is, to a great extent, a pattern of complex association and suggestion which the abstract system of strict allegory cannot accommodate."[2] But an intellectually sophisticated attitude towards
chastity does not imply irony, only a more sophisticated allegorical reading. The Elder Brother is indeed overconfident and the
power of chastity is indeed limited. Chastity does not triumph
as easily as some readers assume. But at no point in the mask are
we made to feel the power of the opposite force. Comus'
speech is quickly and effectively refuted by the answer of the
Lady. Poetic tension depends on the poet's ability to make us
aware of conflict in our feelings. There is no such conflict within
any of the characters in *Comus*, and consequently no tension
in the poem.

Whatever he may have meant by the allegory (and the agreement among critics is more significant here than their differences), Milton was not troubled by any emotional conflict re-
garding the value of chastity. As a result, the language of *Comus*
is quite different from the highly charged language of *Lycidas* or even of *Paradise Regained*. Only in the lyrics does the
language of *Comus* seem effective; and here, of course, we are
looking for excellence of a different kind than in drama. Its

artistic value may very well lie in its ability to unite various arts, as John Demaray has shown in his recent study: "All elements—songs, dances, settings, costumes, and speeches—together 'speak' the message of the work and so reconcile abstract dogma with pleasurable experience."[3]

The Sonnets represent still another side of Milton, and they differ from *Comus*, for the most part, as much as they differ from the other poems. Most of Milton's sonnets are occasional, and do not offer the modern reader the poetic values that we ordinarily expect from lyric poetry. But at least four sonnets are still read with genuine enjoyment; and I believe that *part* of this enjoyment, or a part of the power of these famous sonnets, is linked to conflicts that are poetically realized.

In what is perhaps the most popular sonnet, "Methought I saw my late espoused saint" (Sonnet XXIII), the conflict between the dream or the hope and the dark reality is obvious. And no further comment is needed to make us aware of how this sharp conflict is realized imaginatively in the powerful line that concludes this sonnet: "I walked, she fled, and day brought back my night."

In another famous sonnet, however, "On the late Massacre in Piedmont" (Sonnet XVIII), Milton's moral doctrine is expressed so strongly that readers overlook the fact that it is the quarrel within the poet, rather than his hatred of the Catholics, that gives the poem its poetic, as distinct from its historical, value. In this poem, therefore, we can see another example of the thesis presented throughout this book—that the art of Milton depends less on the value of his beliefs and more on the conflict that is brought about by the belief. The poem is indeed an outcry against the massacre of the Piedmontese. But it is also a poem about the poet's own struggle to overcome his shock at the ways of God towards His saints.

The dominant theme of this sonnet is usually assumed to be sorrow for the victims and anger at the forces who were responsible for the massacre. But it is worth noting that the poem is not addressed to the perpetrators of the massacre, but to God. It is God who must avenge the murdered Piedmontese and record their groans. It is, above all, God who must provide out of "their martyred blood and ashes" an even greater victory over

the Papacy. And God *must* do this, as the imperative verbs
in the key positions of the poem emphasize, because it is God
who is to blame. If *blame* is too strong a word, one may think of
God as responsible; but in any case, we must remember how
firmly Milton and the Puritans believed in the direct intervention by God in the affairs of men. If God could bring about,
as Milton believed, the victories of Cromwell's armies, why
should He not be held responsible when His saints suffered
defeat? "Their moans/The vales redoubled to the hills, and
they to Heav'n. . . ." It is Heaven who must hear the groans of
the victims. But these groans also express the anguish of the
poet who cannot comprehend why Heaven would allow the
slaughter of those "who kept thy truth . . . of old." The poem
therefore not only demands but prophesies the one action that
can justify God's ways to His faithful:

> Their martyred blood and ashes sow
> O'er all th' Italian fields, where still doth sway
> The triple tyrant. . . .

The greater good must be manifested in a visible sign of God's
grace. If such a sign was made visible to all of Europe in
Cromwell's victories, why should one doubt that a Protestant
upsurge would not occur also in Italy? For every martyred
Waldensian, the converts to Protestantism will "grow/A hun-
dredfold." And because Milton is quite sure of this ultimate
victory, the anger and shock at the massacre are modified by a
confident, almost triumphant tone.

   This assurance of final victory can also be seen, although less
obviously, in the progression of images. The first part of the
poem seems to go downward: from "the Alpine mountains cold"
the victims are "roll'd down the rocks," to become "blood and
ashes." But in this same line (10), their moans have reached
"To Heav'n," which out of the same "blood and ashes" will
cause to "grow" an ever stronger army of true believers who
"Early may fly the Babylonian woe." The final verb "fly" seems
to complete the upward movement. If God, for reasons which in
this poem at least are not questioned, has seen fit to allow
his saints to be hurled down the mountains (and the faith of a

true believer to be momentarily stunned), he will also provide an upward movement to restore both the outward victory and, by the same token, the faith of the poet in divine justice.

The confident tone and masculine vigor, which all readers of the poem have felt, are a reflection of the fact that, at this point in his life, Milton was certain that the New Jerusalem would arrive, perhaps in his lifetime. The year of 1655, when this sonnet was written, marks the high point of Milton's political career and of his political hopes. (The *Second Defence of the English People* was written in 1654, and Hanford suggests that Milton began to retire from public life shortly afterwards.) We all know, of course, how great was his disappointment in 1660, and what the effects of this disappointment were on his great attempt to "justify the ways of God to men." But in this sonnet, perhaps for the last time, the reverses suffered by the good men may shake but do not destroy Milton's faith in the ultimate triumph of the saints.

Interpreted in this way, the final effect of the poem is not a mournful cry for revenge on the part of an English Protestant. It is, instead, a cry for assurance that the inward grace of the true believer will be rewarded by an outward sign of God's favor. The question of Milton's attitude towards the Papacy and the Puritan revolution is no longer relevant. We need only participate in the struggle of a man who tests the strength of his convictions against the ways of God. By carefully following the downward and upward movement of the images, we are made aware of the grief that is suggested by the assonance, as well as the strength that is part of the rhythm. By bringing us into his own struggle to justify God's ways by looking towards the future, Milton has made us conscious of those basic emotions that outlast all religious and political controversies.

NOTES

1. To Robert M. Adams and Marjorie Nicolson the poem is essentially a *Mask,* as it was originally entitled, and is less profound than other critics would have us believe. D. C. Allen, as the title of his article, "Milton's *Comus* as a Failure in Artistic Compromise," *ELH* XVI (1949) , 104–109;. indicates, finds that *Comus* is a failure because it attempts to combine the

moral and the dramatic. The majority of the critics, however, see a serious religious and philosophic allegory in this masque. See particularly, A. S. P. Woodhouse, "The Argument in Milton's *Comus*," *UTQ* XI (1941), 47–71; and Sears Jayne, "The Subject of Milton's Ludlow Mask," *PMLA* LXXIV (1959), 533–43 (reprinted in Barker). For full entries of these works see Bibliography.

2. *Poems of Mr. John Milton*, eds. Cleanth Brooks and John E. Hardy (New York, 1951), p. 188.

3. *Milton and the Masque Tradition* (Cambridge, Mass., 1968), p. 142.

Bibliography

Abrams, M. H. "Five Types of Milton's *Lycidas.*" In *Milton's 'Lycidas':
The Tradition and the Poem*, ed. C. A. Patrides. New York, 1961.
Adams, Robert M. *Milton and the Modern Critics*. Ithaca, New York, 1955.
Allen, Don Cameron. "Milton's *Comus* as a Failure in Artistic Compro-
mise." *ELH* XVI (1949) : 104–19.
————. *The Harmonious Vision*. Baltimore, 1954.
Barker, Arthur. "The Pattern of Milton's Nativity Ode." *University of
Toronto Quarterly* X (1941), 167–81.
Broadbent, J. B. "Milton's Mortal Voice and his Omnific Word." In
Approaches to Paradise Lost, ed. C. A. Patrides. London, 1968.
Brockbank, Philip. "Within the Visible Diurnal Sphere: The Moving World
of *Paradise Lost.*" In *Approaches to Paradise Lost*, ed. C. A. Patrides.
London, 1968.
Brooks, Cleanth and Hardy, John E., eds. *Poems of Mr. John Milton: the
1645 Edition with Essays in Analysis*. New York, 1951.
Bush, Douglas, ed. *The Complete Poetical Works of John Milton*. Boston,
1965.
Chambers, A. B. "Wisdom and Fortitude in *Samson Agonistes.*" *PMLA*
LXXVIII (1963), 315–20.
Cope, Jackson I. *The Metaphoric Structure of Paradise Lost*. Baltimore,
1962.
Daniells, Roy. *Milton, Mannerism and Baroque*. Toronto, 1963.
Dewey, John. *Art As Experience*. New York, 1934.
Eliot, T. S. *The Use of Poetry and the Use of Criticism*. New York, 1933.
Ferry, Anne Davidson. *The Narrator in Paradise Lost*. Cambridge, Massa-
chusetts, 1963.
Finney, Gretchen. *Musical Backgrounds for English Literature (1580–1660)*.
New Brunswick, New Jersey, 1962.
Fish, Stanley. *The Reader in Paradise Lost*. New York, 1967.
————. "Question and Answer in *Samson Agonistes.*" *The Critical Quart-
erly* (Autumn, 1969) : 237–64.
Fraser, G. L. "Approaches To '*Lycidas*'." In *The Living Milton: Essays by
Various Hands*, ed. Frank Kermode. London, 1960.
French, Roberts. "Voice and Structure in *Lycidas.*" *Texas Studies In
Literature and Language* XII (Spring, 1970) : 15–25.

123

Frye, Northrop. *The Return of Eden.* Toronto, 1965.

Gardner, Helen. *A Reading of Paradise Lost.* Toronto, 1965.

Hanford, James Holly. "*Samson Agonistes* and Milton in Old Age." Reprinted in *John Milton, Poet and Humanist.* Cleveland, 1966.

————. "The Pastoral Elegy and Milton's *Lycidas*." In *Milton's 'Lycidas': The Tradition and the Poem.* New York, 1961.

Hirsh, E. D., Jr. *Validity in Interpretation.* New Haven, 1967.

Hughes, Merritt Y. "The Christ of *Paradise Regained* and the Renaissance Heroic Tradition." *Studies in Philology* XXV (1938), pp. 254–71.

————. *John Milton, Prose Selections.* New York, 1947.

Jayne, Sears. "The Argument of Milton's *Comus*." *PMLA* LXXIV (1959): 533–43.

Kermode, Frank, ed. *The Living Milton: Essays by Various Hands.* London, 1960.

————. *The Sense of an Ending.* New York, 1967.

Krieger, Murray. "Literary Analysis and Evaluation—and the Ambidextrous Critic." *Contemporary Literature* 9 (Summer 1968), 290–318.

Lewalski, Barbara. *Milton's Brief Epic.* Providence, Rhode Island, 1966.

————. "Innocence and Experience in Milton's Eden." In *New Essays on Paradise Lost.* Berkeley and Los Angeles, 1949.

Lovejoy, A. O. *Essays in the History of Ideas.* Baltimore, 1948.

Low, Anthony. "Action and Suffering: *Samson Agonistes* and the Irony of Alternatives." *PMLA* 84 (1969), 514–19.

MacCaffrey, Isabel Gamble. *Paradise Lost as "Myth."* Cambridge, Massachusetts, 1959.

————. *Samson Agonistes and the Shorter Poems of Milton.* New York, 1967.

Madsen, William, "From Shadowy Types to Truth." In *The Lyric and Dramatic Milton,* ed. Joseph H. Summers. New York, 1965.

More, Paul Elmer. "How to Read *Lycidas*." In *Milton's 'Lycidas': The Tradition and the Poem,* ed. C. A. Patrides. New York, 1961.

Nelson, Lowry, Jr. *Baroque Lyric Poetry.* New Haven, Connecticut, 1961.

Nicolson, Marjorie. *John Milton, A Reader's Guide to His Poetry.* New York, 1963.

————. *Science and Imagination.* Ithaca, New York, 1956.

Patrick, J. Max. *The Prose of John Milton.* Garden City, New York, 1967.

Patrides, C. A., ed. *Milton's 'Lycidas': The Tradition and the Poem.* New York, 1961.

————., ed. *Approaches to Paradise Lost.* London, 1968.

Prince, F. T., ed. *Samson Agonistes.* London, 1957.

Robertson, Duncan. "The Dichotomy of Form and Content." *College English* 28 (January, 1967), 273–79.

Robson, W. W. "The Better Fortitude." In *The Living Milton: Essays by Various Hands.* ed. Frank Kermode. London, 1960.

Ross, Malcolm MacKenzie. *Poetry and Dogma.* New Brunswick, New Jersey, 1954.

Shumaker, Wayne. *Unpremeditated Verse.* Princeton, 1967.

Stapleton, Lawrence. "Milton and the New Music." *University of Toronto Quarterly* XXIII (1953–54), 217–26.

Stein, Arnold. *Answerable Style.* Minneapolis, 1953.

————. *Heroic Knowledge.* Minneapolis, 1957.

Tillyard, E. M. W. *Studies in Milton*. London, 1951.
Tuve, Rosemond. *Images and Themes in Five Poems of Milton*. Cambridge, Massachusetts, 1957.
Waldock, A. J. A. *Paradise Lost and Its Critics*. Cambridge, 1947.
Walsh, Dorothy. *Literature and Knowledge*. Middletown, Connecticut, 1969.
Wittreich, Joseph Anthony, Jr. "Milton's 'Destined Urn': The Art of *Lycidas*." *PMLA* 84 (January 1969), 66–70.
Woodhouse, A. S. P. "The Argument in Milton's *Comus*." *University of Toronto Quarterly* XI (1941), 47–71.
————. "Notes on Milton's Early Development." *University of Toronto Quarterly* XIII (1943), 66–101.
————. "The Theme and Pattern of *Paradise Regained*." *University of Toronto Quarterly* XXX (1956), 167–82.

Index

Abrams, M. H., 21
Allen, Don Cameron, on Samson's use of strength, 107
Areopagitica, 46, 58
astronomy,˙Milton's use of, 48-49

Barker, Arthur, biographical critic of Milton, 12
Brockbank, Philip, on cyclical rhythm of light and darkness in Milton, 39-40
Brooks, Cleanth, 4, 27; ambivalence in Milton's religious feelings, 3; dramatic irony and tension in *Comus*, 118; on Milton's pagan vs. Christian poetic tensions, 14; on the vision of promise and hope in *Lycidas*, 30
Brooks, Cleanth and Hardy, John E. See Brooks, Cleanth
Bush, Douglas, Christ's divinity and humanity contrasted, 90; on Samson's request for guidance, 95; on Satan's tragic potentialities, 41

Christ, and military spirit, 77-78; Milton's possible view of his role, 68; non-human sexual qualities increases distance from us, 80-81
Christian myth, use of by Milton rather than Christian theology, 56
Christian myth and Christian theology, compared, 56-57
Cope, Jackson I., 4; on Satan, 41; rhythmical use of antithetical elements by Milton, 39
Copernican system, and *Paradise Lost*, 49

Daniells, Roy, Satan's exercise of unity, power and will, 40
Demaray, John, reconciliation of dogma and pleasure in *Comus*, 119
Diodati, Charles, Milton's comments to on the *Nativity Ode*, 10

Elegia Quinta, 12
Elegia Sexta, Latin epistle to Charles Diodati containing clues to the *Nativity Ode*, 10

126